D0475477

ZEN

ZEN: Tradition and Transition

EDITED BY

Kenneth Kraft

GROVE PRESS

New York

Published by Grove Press
a division of Wheatland Corporation
920 Broadway
New York, N.Y. 10010

Library of Congress Cataloging-in-Publication Data

Zen: tradition and transition/edited by Kenneth Kraft.—1st ed.
p. cm.
Bibliography: p.
Includes index.
ISBN 0-8021-1022-3
1. Zen Buddhism. I. Kraft, Kenneth Lewis. II. Title: Zen.
BQ9266.Z463 1988 87-34594
294.3'927—dc19 CIP

Designed by Irving Perkins Associates
Manufactured in the United States of America
First Edition 1988
10 9 8 7 6 5 4 3 2 1

The editor wishes to thank the many people who have contributed to this book. Philip Kapleau and Martin Collcutt gave steady encouragement and sound advice. Hori Sōgen, Zenson Gifford, Margaret Case, Alan Sponberg, Dale Saunders, William Tyler, and Jerome Packard made insightful comments on portions of the manuscript. Jeanette MacNeille cheerfully put the text on a disc. Myokyo-ni, Tom Roberts, Lea Liu, and Trudy Kraft provided other kinds of valuable assistance. The project has been expertly guided to completion by Hannelore Rosset and Fred Jordan.

Contents

Note to the Reader

Some readers may be wary of the many non-English words that tend to crop up when Zen is discussed. In the following pages the use of unfamiliar proper names and technical terms has been restricted, though in certain contexts (such as the history of Zen in Asia) they cannot be avoided. Except for widely recognized words like satori or karma, most foreign terms are italicized and defined briefly on their first appearance in each chapter; subsequent appearances in that chapter are not italicized. Ch'an (the Chinese pronunciation of "Zen") is the name of the Zen school in China; some authors maintain the distinction, while others use "Zen" to refer to Chinese Ch'an as well as Japanese Zen. The names of Chinese Zen masters may appear in two forms in this book, either according to the Chinese or the Japanese pronunciation. They are cross-referenced in the Index. In Chinese and Japanese, one's surname precedes one's given name, unless the name is better known in another order, such as D. T. Suzuki. The Japanese title "Roshi" (Zen teacher or master), used here without italics or macron, is placed after Japanese names but before the names of some Americans, in accord with individual preference. Plurals of transliterated foreign words are handled as English plurals ("koans"), following the custom of American practitioners.

Introduction

by Kenneth Kraft

> One night I took up the *Lotus Sutra*. Suddenly I penetrated to the perfect, true, ultimate meaning of the *Lotus*. The doubts I had held initially were destroyed, and I became aware that the understanding I had obtained up to then was greatly in error. Unconsciously I uttered a great cry and burst into tears.[1]
>
> —HAKUIN EKAKU

> One day I was reading one of these [Zen] letters in a car going to work—I was in a car pool, and my office was about an hour from the Zen Center—and a powerful opening occurred right in the car, much more powerful than the first. One phrase triggered it, and all my questions were resolved. I couldn't stop laughing or crying, both at once, and the people in the car were very upset and concerned, they didn't have any idea what was happening, and I kept telling them there was nothing to worry about![2]
>
> —BERNARD GLASSMAN

These two enlightenment experiences are separated by some two hundred and fifty years. In the first, dated 1718, the speaker is a Japanese Zen monk in his early thirties; in the second, the speaker is an American mathematician and Zen practitioner of about the same age. Despite the discrepancies of time and culture, both men experienced a flash of intuitive insight into the essential nature of all existence, the oneness beyond conceptualization. In Zen terms, they became linked with all those who had similarly awakened before them, "seeing with the same eyes and hearing with the same ears."

While Zen's origins go back more than a thousand years to remote mountain sites in China, it is still practiced today in many parts of the world by people from all walks of life. Descendants of ancient religious lineages continue to teach its classic doctrines and methods, preserving systems of training which hold out a remarkable promise—that the same enlightenment realized by the great masters of the past can become an actual fact of one's own experience. Zen nurtures a deep reverence for tradition, and at the same time it promotes a high degree of spontaneity and flexible adaptation. It thus remains vital through change. The present volume is subtitled "Tradition and Transition" because it encompasses these two dimensions—a time-honored core and its continuing evolution, as represented by the Japanese monk and the American practitioner.

For Zen masters and scholars to cooperate in producing an inclusive one-volume work on Zen is itself a notable departure. Generally the subject is tackled either from an internal standpoint by committed adherents or from an external standpoint by more neutral observers. Practitioners tend to read the great Zen masters or the Buddhist sutras and shy away from academic treatises, while university students are usually assigned descriptive and analytical works by scholars, with a sprinkling of translated source materials that are often read out of context. This book has been written to help bridge the gap between these customary approaches, by specialists interested in reexamining the relation between the study and practice of Zen.

Throughout Zen's history, Buddhist scholars and Zen masters have eyed each other warily, and their encounters often resulted in dramatic "Dharma duels." One of the essays in this volume recounts an anecdote from ninth-century China, in which Zen master Lung-tan has a long discussion with Te-shan, a scholar-monk renowned for his commentaries on the *Diamond Sutra*:

> [S]ince Te-shan was considered an authority on this scripture, lecturing widely on it, we can presume he questioned the master about it at great length and received the sort of responses that left him suspended in mid-air. When Lung-tan finally said, "It is getting late, you had better leave," Te-shan's mind was emptied of all the concepts he had been harboring. Peering out, he said, "It's dark outside." Thereupon the master lit a candle and handed it to him. As Te-shan went to take it, Lung-tan suddenly blew it out. With that Te-shan was enlightened.

Even if this cryptic story leaves *us* in the dark, the traditional account goes on to clarify the lesson we are expected to draw. The next day Te-shan burned all his notes and commentaries, declaring:

> Even though one masters various profound teachings, it is like placing a single hair in vast space. Even if one gains all the essential knowledge in the world, it is like throwing a drop of water into a deep ravine.[3]

In its well-known slogans Zen defines itself as "a mind-to-mind transmission" that is "not dependent on words." Zen lore makes the point graphically: an illiterate Sixth Patriarch tears up sutras; Chinese master Ta-hui burns his teacher's compilation of classic anecdotes; Japanese master Kanzan leaves no written trace of his teachings. Understandably, Zen is often depicted as anti-intellectual and antitextual, notions amplified by some of its earliest spokesmen in the West. For example, D. T. Suzuki repeatedly insisted:

> No amount of verbal discussion, therefore, no logical acuteness, no intellectual subtlety will probe the deep secrets of Zen.[4]

Such statements are valid in one sense, yet they are also potentially misleading. Zen recognizes the limitations of thought but does not suppress it. Though learning is never accepted as a substitute for enlightenment, most of the great masters were deeply learned men. As Roshi Philip Kapleau points out herein, the line between "a profound intellectual awareness (based on an experience of insight) and a genuine awakening" can be a fine one. Zen has roots in Indian Buddhism, which recognized three types of religious cognition: preparatory, transcendent, and subsequent. The most important is the second, and it is indeed nonconceptual, but the kinds of understanding that precede and follow a flash of intuitive insight are also essential to the spiritual quest.[5]

Nor is Zen antitextual, in spite of occasional book-burnings by Te-shan and others. Though Zen focuses sharply on the delusive potential of language, it takes its own literature seriously. Several of the following essays reveal the central role played by texts in the tradition's development. Zen's warnings against overreliance on written works often had a political function—the emerging sect needed to distinguish itself from existing Buddhist schools that embraced major sutras. When Zen master Dōgen addressed his own students, he taught that "an enlightened person always masters the sutras to full advantage."[6]

Western practitioners of Zen sometimes interpret its alleged antitextual attitude as a prohibition against all reading, not to mention the academic study of Buddhism. However, in this case *more* study may be needed, because Zen in the West is so detached from Buddhist culture, the larger context of its original Asian setting. Professor Martin Collcutt observes in his epilogue that this lack of background has made it difficult for many Westerners to determine what is essential to Zen practice and to the master's role. Eido Shimano Roshi notes in his essay that Asian monks beginning practice on a Zen *kōan* were traditionally given little or no instruction, while Westerners require some kind of map in such unfamiliar territory. Another contributor quotes the Zen poet Ryōkan on the importance of correct orientation as one embarks on a spiritual journey: "If you point your cart north when you want to go south, how will you arrive?"

In recent years, Western scholars have made significant progress in Zen studies, even allowing Zen to challenge some of the methods and assumptions of their academic disciplines. Not long ago very different attitudes prevailed. In 1931, Sir George Sansom, the distinguished historian of Japan, wondered if Zen wasn't a "sham and pretentious mysticism"; he accused Zen masters of "playing to the gallery" and suggested that meditators just "doze in their seats and think depraved, wanton thoughts."[7] In contrast, the receptivity of a new generation of Zen specialists is seen in the following remarks by Professor John Maraldo:

> [T]he various scholarly approaches we may take toward the study of Zen inevitably reach a point where the object of study turns about and begins to question the approach itself, its vantage point, and its ground. When we study Zen as a phenomenon, we come to a point where Zen reveals itself as the study of phenomena; when we study the history of Zen, Zen begins to question our notions of history; and when we study the philosophical background, logic, and content of Zen, Zen itself elicits a profound reflection on the nature of philosophy.[8]

The interests of the academic and practicing communities most clearly converge in the need for accurate, lively translations, and important works are steadily appearing in several Western languages. Advances in other areas of Zen scholarship, some of which might merit the attention of practitioners, include the following: 1) A treasure-trove of new material on early Ch'an (Zen) in China is coming to light. As Dr. John McRae's chapter demonstrates, our picture of the origins of Zen, including the lives and teachings of such patriarchs as Bodhidharma and Hui-neng, has been significantly revised. 2) Comparative study of Zen and Western thought continues to advance on many fronts. Journal articles pairing Dōgen with Heidegger, Whitehead, or Eckhart abound; American philosophers turn to Buddhist dialectics for new solutions to old problems. 3) For the first time, Zen is being scrutinized using tools from various Western disciplines (with mixed results). For example, Dōgen has recently been interpreted from a phenomenological perspective, and Zen anecdotes have been subjected to linguistic discourse analysis. 4) The writings of the Kyoto School, increasingly available in English and German, are reaching a wider audience. These twentieth-century Japanese philosophers, rooted in Zen but also well-trained in Western intellectual history, offer the Buddhist insight into "absolute nothingness" as an antidote to the current nihilistic impasse they perceive in Western thought and civilization.

The benefits of Zen training cannot be achieved simply through study, but as long as that point is understood then study need not be a hindrance to practice. In proper balance, the two can complement and nurture each other; ideally, a sincere Western student of Zen (or Buddhism) should be exposed to both. In Zen terms, at the level where all activity is seen as Buddha-nature manifesting itself, the distinction between study and practice disappears. Zen master Eisai wrote, " 'Sutras' and 'Zen' are just names; 'practice' and 'study' are also just provisional names."[9] Another master, Musō, reiterated:

> The Buddha did not call himself only a man of doctrine, nor did he call himself only a man of Zen. Nor did he separate his teachings into a doctrine portion and a Zen portion, because Buddha's inner realization cannot be equated with either of them.[10]

Zen adherents living in today's demythologized world will eventually need to clarify some of the sensitive issues raised by the work of scholars, such as the competing claims of historical and religious truth. And scholars must continue their struggle to elucidate Zen without succumbing to cultural, disciplinary, or personal presuppositions. If the cross-fertilization represented by these efforts (and this volume) bears fruit, it may generate new approaches to Zen practice and new approaches to Buddhist scholarship. In Professor Maraldo's vision:

> I ask if Zen itself may be practiced as a field of scholarship, that is, a kind of study which takes the self, life and death, and the entire world as its domain. Zen would then be a discipline in both senses

> of the word: a spiritual *and* intellectual training; and would bear directly on current attempts to resolve the issues of the modern world.[11]

Of the eleven essays that follow, ten were written expressly for this anthology, in response to invitations from the editor.[12] For the academic student of Zen, a wide range is covered—from the earliest texts on Zen meditation to previously untranslated classics of Zen poetry. Several of the chapters incorporate recent findings by scholars that have not yet circulated beyond specialized journals. For a newcomer who is curious about Zen practice, the writers offer instructions on how to meditate and guidelines for identifying a qualified Zen teacher. The practitioner with some experience will find fresh perspectives on the master-disciple encounter and an account that challenges accepted beliefs about the Zen patriarchs. Even advanced practitioners may use this book to test their own understanding against the insights of experienced masters, to enrich their knowledge of the tradition, or to learn about recent developments in other Zen communities.

Though the practice-oriented chapters by the teachers precede the scholars' more historical pieces, no firm boundary divides the two groups or the two approaches. One of the Zen masters holds a Ph.D. and heads an institute of Buddhist studies; another serves as president of a Japanese university. The contributing scholars have all been exposed to Zen training at some point, and several remain committed to their personal practice. Thus the masters at times write in a scholarly vein, and the scholars often articulate matters of deep concern to practitioners.

Personal experience is primary in Zen. Chapter 1, by Morinaga Sōkō Roshi, is an intimate account of his early experiences as a Zen novice in Japan. During World War II, Morinaga at the age of nineteen was about to fly a suicide mission as a *kamikaze* pilot when the war ended abruptly. He tells how, shortly thereafter, he found his way to the entrance hall of a Zen monastery and describes the ordeal of gaining admission as a monk. Today

Morinaga is abbot of his former master's temple, Daishuin, and honorary president of Hanazono University, affiliated with the Rinzai sect of Japanese Zen. He has also guided many Western students of Zen.

Seated meditation (*zazen*) is the heart of Zen training, the practice that gives the tradition its name. In the second chapter, Master Sheng-Yen traces the pre-Zen origins of zazen and distinguishes the Zen approach to meditation from similar disciplines. His practical instructions for a novice cover posture, breathing, and the focus of attention. These criteria for correct zazen, he asserts, "have not changed since ancient days." A Ch'an (Zen) monk since the age of thirteen, Sheng-Yen is director of the Chung-Hwa Institute of Buddhist Studies in Taiwan and founder of the Ch'an Meditation Center in Elmhurst, New York.

Like zazen, the one-on-one encounter with the Zen master is an essential feature of Zen training. In Chapter 3, Roshi Kapleau provides a teacher's view of this encounter, drawing on his thirteen years as a Zen practitioner in Japan and his twenty years as spiritual director of the Zen Center of Rochester, New York. Some of Kapleau's disclosures are unprecedented in written accounts of Zen—for instance, how a teacher tests students to determine whether they have experienced genuine enlightenment. He also addresses certain objections that are commonly raised about Zen training, such as its alleged severity.

Zen koans are existential conundrums with a resolution lying beyond the intellect; they are the subject of the following chapter by Eido Roshi. Eido outlines the traditional Japanese koan system with its ascending categories, but he also questions its applicability for the West. In an experimental spirit, he offers a number of koan-like passages from classic Western sources that he believes could form the basis of a new collection for Zen practitioners in Europe and America. Trained in the Japanese Rinzai sect, Eido has been teaching Zen in America for over twenty years. He is abbot of the Zen Studies Society, based in New York City.

In Chapter 5, the Canadian Zen teacher Albert Low offers an

essay on one of the best-known texts in the Zen tradition, a verse in praise of meditation by the Japanese master Hakuin Ekaku. Low demonstrates the spirited style of Zen commentary, which is neither literary nor philosophical. He addresses a question often heard: "Are we retreating from the world's problems or our own through the practice of Zen?" A devotee of Zen since 1961, Low completed his formal training with Roshi Kapleau. Currently he is director and teacher at the Montreal Zen Centre.

With Dr. Burton Watson's chapter on Zen poetry, the volume shifts to more scholarly assessments of Zen. One of the most distinguished translators of works in Chinese and Japanese, Watson shows that Zen has been linked closely to poetry over the centuries. The verses range from those on enlightenment and death to light-hearted haiku about public bathing. Watson acknowledges that a considerable amount of Zen poetry is not outstanding (judged strictly as poetry), but he argues that the work of poets such as Han-shan and Ryōkan achieves indisputable distinction. Watson translated the verses in his essay expressly for this volume.

The next three chapters trace the historical development of Zen in China and Japan. Dr. McRae, of Harvard University's Fairbank Center for East Asian Research, focuses on one of the most famous stories in early Zen: the poetry contest used to select Zen's Sixth Patriarch. Challenging the historicity of the traditional account, McRae reconstructs the actual origins of the Zen school in China. In the process he reveals what we really know about the Sixth Patriarch—almost nothing. Nonetheless, McRae concludes that vital aspects of Zen are expressed in this seminal legend.

In Chapter 8, Professor Philip Yampolsky of Columbia University surveys Zen history in Japan from the pioneers of the twelfth century through Hakuin, who did so much to revive Zen in the eighteenth century. Though some of the first Zen spokesmen in the West portrayed Zen as standing outside history, Yampolsky identifies major figures, traces various lineages, and notes the cycles of degeneration and renewal. New light is shed on the role of Nōnin, a self-proclaimed Zen master whose teachings were controversial during a formative period. Yampolsky, an expert in both Chinese and Japanese Zen, is recognized as the dean of American Zen scholars.

The story of Japanese Zen is brought up to date by Professor T. Griffith Foulk of the University of Michigan. Foulk outlines the daily life of Zen monks today and clarifies the differences between the Rinzai and Sōtō sects. He argues that Japanese Zen is very much in the Buddhist mainstream, citing the many features that Zen rituals share with other Buddhist schools and noting the importance of funeral services as a source of income. Foulk's institutional focus calls into question certain widely held notions about Zen.

Zen was first introduced to the West in the late nineteenth century; in the past two decades numerous centers have been established in North America and Europe. The editor's chapter on recent developments in North American Zen describes the struggle to adapt Zen training to the needs of laypeople, the unprecedented participation of women, and the new generation of teachers. Though Zen in America suffered a recession in the early 1980s, beset by internal and external difficulties, signs of renewed vitality are visible. What are Zen's future prospects in its new Western setting?

One aspect of Zen's acculturation in the West that perplexes many practitioners is the nature and extent of a Zen master's authority, especially in the crucial master-disciple relationship. Professor Collcutt of Princeton University reflects upon this issue in his epilogue. Though trust in the teacher is indispensable to Zen training, Collcutt argues that common sense and basic moral standards cannot be abandoned in the search for an authentic spiritual guide or in the leadership of a Buddhist community.

In Zen centers across North America today there is growing awareness that Zen is rooted in a vast Buddhist tradition, and that a great deal remains to be learned from that tradition. As a result, practitioners are forming study groups, inviting specialists to lecture, and setting up academic institutes. For over a decade the Zen Center of Los Angeles has been affiliated with the Kuroda Institute for the Study of Buddhism and Human Values; their conferences and publications have noticeably strengthened Buddhist studies in the West. In the spring of 1986, the Rochester Zen Center hosted a conference of Buddhist scholars to mark its twentieth anniversary. That summer the Zen Lotus Society in Ann Arbor organized a week-long gathering of Zen teachers and scholars from the United States and Canada. The five Zen masters and the six Zen scholars who joined together in creating this book have added their voices to this open-minded and open-ended dialogue.

1. My Struggle to Become a Zen Monk

by Morinaga Sōkō

I was born in Uotsu, on the Japan Sea, and was a liberal arts student at Toyama High School when the Second World War was at its height. At first all high-school pupils were exempt from conscription until they left school. However, when the war situation worsened an imperial edict was issued summoning liberal arts students to the front. Apparently the reasoning behind this was that science pupils might make a positive contribution to the war by their future study of medicine and the natural sciences, whereas liberal arts pupils were more likely to upset the national spirit with their argumentative theories.

All of us know that we will die someday—perhaps tomorrow, perhaps in twenty or thirty years time. What makes life and peace of mind possible is the fact that we do not really know when death will come. But awaiting the arrival of our call-up papers, we students suddenly felt we were staring death in the face. Every day I seemed to be treading air. Whether awake or asleep I kept thinking about my own death in action. But it was too late to look for philosophical or religious answers to the question of death. The young men who entered the services found a makeshift answer to their misgivings by blindly convincing themselves that it was a just war for which they could not begrudge the sacrifice of their own lives. I did so too.

We believed that the economically developed nations of Europe and America had been exploiting the East for a long time. Our country had risen up against this oppression and was waging a just and meaningful war of liberation, a cause which well merited, if need be, our own bodies being smashed to pieces. So my classmates and friends climbed into airplanes fueled for a one-way mission to certain death. With their favorite philosophy book or Shinran's *Passages Deploring Deviations of Faith* (*Tannishō*)[1] placed beside their joysticks, they went off to plunge down on the enemy ships. Many of them were shot down and crashed into the sea before they could accomplish their mission.

After Japan's unconditional surrender on August 15, 1945, we were told our country had conducted a war of aggression and evil, and that the war leaders were to be executed. The end of the war found me still alive, and I was soon demobilized. Somehow I got hold of a multiband radio and listened to broadcasts about the German war trials. Even now I can hear ringing in my ears the echo of that voice pronouncing the words ". . . to be hanged." Newsreels were also shown, probably a policy determined by the American army of occupation. I could not help but feel sickened by the sight of German generals hanged in the public square amidst the stares of huge crowds, and by the scenes of the Italian leader Mussolini and his lover dangling head down from a wire noose and then being dragged around the streets with everyone cursing them and hurling stones.

One by one we students returned to school, clad in government surplus uniforms. But for all of us who had lived until then with no firm beliefs the big question was how to distinguish between good and evil. We pondered and discussed this matter day after day. In the aftermath of the war the Japanese had completely lost sight of an ethical standard. We no longer even knew how best to bring up our children.

The year before the war ended I had lost both my parents at one blow. The shock of my mother's death proved too great for my seriously ill father; he died in a coma the following morning. My call-up papers had already arrived, and I had barely two days in which to rush the funeral through and settle my affairs before I entered the army. For generations my family had been landowners and had let the small amount of land we possessed to tenant farmers. Father used to say to me, "There is nothing more reliable than land. Fire won't burn it, floods won't wash it away, and robbers can't carry it off. So whatever you do at least make sure you don't part with the land." But the post-war Land Reform Program took the family land away. There was nothing left I could trust. All I had believed to be secure turned out to be transitory.

Further, as a result of a post-war measure to freeze bank deposits, not a yen was available from the insurance my father had bought to safeguard his children. Yet prices rose rapidly: what could be bought one day for one yen cost ten the next day and soon after one hundred. As students in those days did not do part-time work, I had no idea how to go about earning money with my own two hands. So I had lost both an ethical standard by which to live and the financial means with which to support myself. In my utter misery, it would not have been surprising if I had joined some gang of criminals or hurled myself under a train. Though I managed to finish high school, I felt no inclination to go on to a university. Instead, I just idled away my time, feeling miserable. After quite a while it suddenly struck me that the real reason I no longer knew what to do with my life was that I had only read books and theorized about things, without ever imposing any discipline upon myself.

Finding a Zen Master

This strange set of circumstances eventually prompted me to knock at the gates of several Zen temples. One day I was led to Gotō Zuigan Roshi, master of Daishuin temple in Kyoto. He had been head abbot of Myōshinji temple and later of Daitokuji temple and had now retired. I presented myself before him sloppily dressed, with unkempt hair. His first words were, "Why have you come here?" In reply I went on and on about everything that had happened to me. The Roshi heard me out in silence for over an hour without once interrupting. When I had gotten it all off my chest, he said, "I've listened to what you've said, and it seems to me you've lost faith in everything and everybody. However, Zen training is impossible if you don't trust your teacher. Can you trust me? If you can I'll take you on just as you are. If you can't it would be a waste of time, and you'd be better off going home."

I think in our present society we have forgotten that when it comes to learning something, trust in one's teacher is absolutely essential, whether he is a Zen master or a university professor. So it was the first thing the Roshi emphasized. However, I was a complete good-for-nothing without integrity. Despite the Roshi's venerable seventy years of age, I thought to myself, "This silly old man may well have been the abbot of Myōshinji and Daitokuji for all I care, but the world is full of imposters in high positions. How can he expect me to put my whole trust in him? I have only just met him. If it were that simple, I would have trusted someone or believed something before and need not to have come here." However, the most important thing then was to be allowed to stay, even if it meant lying. So I said, "I trust you, please take me on."

"Come along with me," the Roshi said. The first task I was given was to sweep the garden with a bamboo broom. If we are honest we have to admit that our innermost motives are often extremely petty. While still thinking him a silly old man for expecting me to trust him, I somehow wanted to win the Roshi's approval. So I grasped my broom and swept mightily and soon had a mountain of leaves. I asked, "Roshi, where should I put all this rubbish?" hoping he would see how good I had been. He immediately roared, "Leaves are not rubbish!" I started to say, "That's all very well but over here . . ." He replied, "You don't trust me, do you? Go to the shed and bring any empty charcoal sacks you find there." Coming back, I found the Roshi vigorously raking through the pile of leaves so that any stones or gravel fell to the bottom. He then took the sacks and filled them to the very last leaf, packing them tightly with his feet. "Now go put these back in the shed," he said, "They're kindling for the bath fire."

When I carried the sacks back to the shed I realized that the leaves were not rubbish after all, but I was still convinced that the remaining bits and pieces were. However, when I came back I saw the Roshi squatting on the ground picking out the small stones from what remained. When he had carefully gathered them together to the last tiny pebble, he said, "Now put these beneath the eaves." The raindrops dripping from the roof had made depressions in the gravel beneath the eaves, and I used the pebbles to fill these holes. I had to admit to myself that the stones looked attractive there, but I was still quite sure that the remaining lumps of earth and scraps of moss could serve no useful purpose. Yet the Roshi just collected them together without fuss and placed them on the palm of his hand. Searching patiently, he put the lumps of earth into depressions in the ground, then firmed them in with his foot until nothing remained. He said, "Now do you understand a little? Originally, there is no rubbish in either men or things." This was the first teaching I received from Zuigan Roshi.

The Roshi's words that originally there is no rubbish either in men or in things actually comprise the basic truth of Buddhism. According to traditional accounts, the Buddha taught, "How marvelous, how wonderful! All sentient beings are perfect and without flaw. It is only due to delusive attachments that the truth cannot be seen." These are the famous words spoken by Shakyamuni at the moment of his enlightenment. In another version he also said, "I attained the Way simultaneously with the whole world and with all sentient beings. Everything—mountains, rivers, trees, grasses—all attained buddhahood." At the moment when the fog clouding his own eyes cleared, the Enlightened One's voice rang out, "I believed that all things in this world lived in a wretched condition of suffering, but now I see that all beings are Buddha and are without the slightest flaw. Not only those blessed with a healthy body but those who cannot see, or who have lost their hands, or who are lame, they too are perfect just the way they are." So from the very beginning Zuigan Roshi had pointed out for me the root of the Great Matter, though I was too dull-witted to understand.

Gradually I realized that trusting meant to trust without a murmur of dissent. I must say "Yes, yes!" to everything I was told. Therefore, even when told to do three things at once or to do something I had never done before, I was never to say "I can't do it" or "I don't know how to do it." Rather, it was up to me to find out how to accomplish whatever I was given to do, taxing my resources and ingenuity to the utmost. The Roshi's words to me about trusting one's master also meant working it out for myself without complaint.

During that first day I was also told to wipe the wooden corridors. I duly got down on my hands and knees, cloth in hand, and swished left and right. But the corridors in a temple are different from those of ordinary houses. "Idiot!" the Roshi shouted. "How many days do you think you're going to spend doing that? I'll show you how it's done." Then I saw the seventy-year-old master speeding along on all fours, cloth pressed on the floor with his hands, bottom thrust in the air. At that sight scales dropped from my eyes. I had known nothing but theorizing; during my high school days I often spent the whole night with friends reading books on philosophy and arguing—talk, talk, talk. I now burned with shame because I could not even do such a simple job as cleaning a floor properly.

These days, too, when bright young people from first-rate universities come to my temple to practice *zazen* (seated meditation), the first task I assign them is heating the bath. But the fire has been lit under an empty bathtub so many times that I now query beforehand, "What's the first thing you do when you heat a bath?" "Light the fire," they reply. "Jolly well not!" I say. "Fill it with water," they then reply. So I explain that first they should clean the tub, then fill it with water, then check the water level, then cover the top of the tub with the wooden lid, and only then kindle the fire underneath. But when I go to check how they are getting on, I find one or two large logs and lots of burnt newspaper. "That won't burn! Use some kindling!" "But there isn't any kindling," they reply. "Then chop some." "I don't know where the hatchet is." "Well, why don't you ask someone?" Finally they set about splitting kindling. However, as I half expect, the fire still does not burn properly. Peering inside, I find they have not removed the old ashes. So I ask again, "What makes a fire burn?" and the reply comes back, "A chemical combination of matter and oxygen." "Well, if that's the case, why don't you remove these ashes and let some air in? And while you're about it, you'd better clean the chimney too." They duly climb onto the roof to clean the bathhouse chimney, and on their way down, as sure as not, they chip a few roof tiles. However, I cannot laugh at these young people, because when I first came to Daishuin I was just like them.

Though I continued pretending outwardly to be a disciple who trusted his master, in my heart I criticized him and rebelled against him. In fact, many of the things he said made me seethe with anger, such as his comments to his attendant during tea sessions. In a small Zen temple like Daishuin the breakfast of rice gruel is followed by formal tea served in the Roshi's room. After the Roshi has been served, the others also have tea while listening to his plans for the day. When I first came to Daishuin an old lady named Miss Okamoto also lived there. She was a graduate of the well-known Ochanomizu Ladies College and for many years had been involved with women's education. In her forties she had become deeply devoted to Buddhism and to the Roshi; she gave up her teaching appointment to spend the rest of her life taking care of his personal needs. At that time just the three of us lived in the temple together. The Roshi used to talk to Miss Okamoto, but he never said a word to me. One morning, probably taking pity on me, she said, "And what do you think, Morinaga?" She was trying to draw me into the conversation. But before I could reply the Roshi said, "No, no! He's not yet fit to talk in front of people."

From the Roshi's standpoint, you had first to know yourself before you were qualified to talk in the company of others. In Zen terms, this "knowing yourself" is called *kenshō,* which means to have clearly seen and verified one's true nature. And since I had not done so, I was not to speak.

Between Master and Disciple

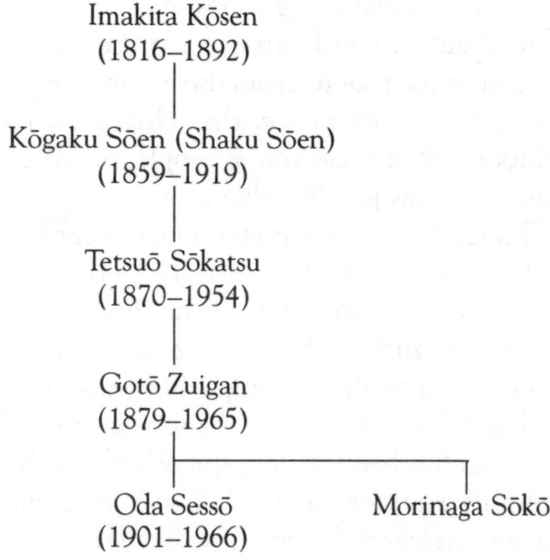

At the bottom of the chart you will see my name, Sōkō, and that of my senior Dharma brother, Sessō. Our teacher was Zuigan Roshi, and Zuigan Roshi's teacher was Sōkatsu Roshi. In this way, from master to master, we trace our Zen lineage back to Shakyamuni Buddha. *Inka* is the seal of the authentic transmission of Dharma, which is the Law of the universe and the teaching of Shakyamuni. Only those who have received this seal from their teachers, as acknowledgment of their spiritual insight, are recorded in such a genealogy. In the Rinzai sect, such people are accorded the honorific title of roshi.

Imakita Kōsen Roshi, at the top of the chart, was the distinguished head abbot of Engakuji temple in Kamakura in the mid-nineteenth century. During the anti-Buddhist movement of the 1870s, the first years of the Meiji period, he made great efforts to promote a nonsectarian form of Buddhism. The layman D.T. Suzuki, an ardent admirer, wrote a book about him called *Imakita Kōsen*. The Dharma heir of Kōsen Roshi was Sōen Roshi, who was the first Japanese master to take Zen to America and who also became head abbot of Engakuji. Some famous novelists and other influential people trained under him.

One morning at formal tea Miss Okamoto asked Zuigan Roshi, "Roshi, who was greater, Kōsen Roshi or his heir Sōen Roshi?" Zuigan Roshi was a very solemn man not likely to make jokes. He replied soberly, "Master Kōsen was greater." Miss Okamoto then asked, "Who was greater, Sōen Roshi or his heir Sōkatsu Roshi?" Sōkatsu Roshi had no desire to become head abbot of a famous monastery; after receiving inka he settled in a small Tokyo temple and accepted laypeople for training. Zuigan Roshi replied, "Master Sōen was greater." When Miss Okamoto heard this, she said, "But Roshi, doesn't that mean that the lineage is getting weaker? Well then, who is greater, your teacher Sōkatsu Roshi or you?" In a flash the reply came back, "I am greater." When Zuigan Roshi replied in dead earnest that he was greater than his own teacher, Miss Okamoto was greatly pleased. But when I heard her ask, "Roshi, who is now greater, you or your disciple Sessō?" I almost burst out laughing.

At that time, Zuigan Roshi had reached the pinnacle of the Zen world, having been successively head abbot of Myōshinji and Daitokuji, whereas Sessō, without any position as yet, was caretaker of a small sub-temple within the grounds of Myōshinji. Since I had no insight into a man's true nature but judged people solely by their social standing, I could not help thinking how absurd it was to try and compare Sessō with Zuigan Roshi, and I tried hard to contain my laughter. But without a moment's reflection Zuigan Roshi replied, "It is not yet known!" At those words the laughter suddenly died in me and tears welled up in my eyes. I realized what a splendid teacher I had. Although he would invariably take the hard line and say, "That fellow is not fit to talk in front of people," Zuigan Roshi always bore in mind a disciple's future development. He took into account not just the disciple's present immature form, but also the form he was confident the disciple would have after one, two, ten, or twenty years of training. This was the implication of his words, "It is not yet known," which struck me so forcibly. Indeed, almost as though confirming his words, Sessō later succeeded Zuigan as head abbot of Daitokuji. I also trained under Sessō Roshi, and he was the equal of his teacher in every way. From that moment I began to feel a deep trust in my teacher, but I still lacked even the slightest understanding.

At one point in my training I did something wrong, and Master Zuigan, in accord with custom, ordered me to leave Daishuin. When I went to ask forgiveness and permission to stay, prostrating myself with my head to the ground in the required manner, he did not relent. No matter how many times I begged to be allowed to remain his disciple, he countered with a firm "No." Finally, in real despair, I lifted my head from the floor and looked up at the Roshi. When I saw his stern look, a lump rose in my throat. I just stared back at him and out of the very depths of my being stated, "Whatever happens, whatever you say, however you try to throw me out, I'll never leave your side, never, never!" Thus eye to eye with the Roshi, I saw tears form in his eyes, slowly well over, and flow down his cheeks. I was moved to the core of my heart by the bond that I felt with him. I knew that I was truly his disciple for life, and I also knew that he knew it and that he was glad to have such a disciple.

The relationship between master and disciple must be so close and so strong that not even a single hair can be inserted between them. It might be compared with sumo wrestlers in the ring. Huge men weighing over three hundred fifty pounds can crash into their opponents with all their might only because they have absolute confidence that the ring in which they fight will not give way beneath them. In Zen training the "I" must at all costs be broken. But this tenacious "I" cannot be conquered in a timid fashion. Nothing will come of the training unless you dig in your heels and hang on despite being scolded, struck, or threatened with expulsion.

I had spent more than a year at Daishuin when the Roshi said to me, "People, especially novice monks, should not live alone. You need to come into contact with many people. Practicing as the only disciple under a teacher is fine, but now you should enter a monastery to interact with others." My training at Daishuin was considered preliminary, and I was still classed as a novice. Properly to become a Zen monk I had to enter a monastery. It was decided then that I should be sent to Daitokuji, one of the largest Zen monasteries in Kyoto, less than an hour's walk from Daishuin.

When setting out for a monastery, you take a *bunko*, a satchel-sized box which contains your monastic robe. A pair of bundles hung from your shoulders hold your other possessions: eating bowls, chopsticks, a whetstone and razor for shaving, sutra books, undergarments, and a raincape. You wear the traditional outfit of leggings, straw sandals, and wicker hat, tucking up the robe with a band.

As I was getting everything together, the Roshi came in and asked, "How are you getting on? Have you packed your bunko yet?" "No, I am just doing it," I replied. "Fine. Bring the lid of your bunko to my room." I did as he asked, wondering what he had in mind. When I handed the lid to him, he stuck three one-thousand yen notes inside. At that time one thousand yen was still a considerable sum of money. He asked, "Do you know what this is for?" When I had first tumbled into Daishuin I had told him that I still had a little of the money my father had left me, so he never once gave me any pocket money. But now that I was off to the monastery, I thought the Roshi had relented and was giving me some. His explanation utterly confounded me. "This is Nirvana money, for the disposal of your corpse. You are on your way to the training monastery. It may cost you your life. Should you have the misfortune to die in a wayside ditch or in the middle of your training, this money is to ensure that your corpse can be disposed of without inconvenience to others." His stern manner made me feel more determined than ever.

During the war, when we students were leaving for the front, I had thought a good deal about death. Yet when the Roshi said, "This money is for the disposal of your corpse," death in this case meant something different. It was not just a question of my physical death, but of the death of "I." However much we may argue otherwise, when it really comes down to it we hold ourselves very dear indeed. Unless we undergo thorough training to wean ourselves from this stubborn attachment to "I," our inherent wisdom is clouded and our inherent compassion is blocked. These days, when I in my turn send a disciple off to a monastery, I supply several ten-thousand yen notes for the disposal of his corpse.

Very early the next morning, in the darkness before dawn, I went to Zuigan Roshi's room. "With your permission, I am now leaving," I said. I made my way to the kitchen entrance and stepped down onto the dirt floor; as a novice, I was not permitted to use the main entrance. While tying on my sandals, I was startled to see that the Roshi had followed me. He was a proud man, not likely to come and see a young novice off. Yet he stepped down onto the dirt floor. Squatting down at my feet, he began to tie the cords of my straw sandals for me. Thoroughly embarrassed, I protested, "It's all right, I can do it myself," and tried to draw my feet away. But he firmly took hold of them. "Come on, give over," he said. Having tied the strings, he tapped the knots and declared, "You are never to undo these!" Of course I would have to untie them to enter the monastery, but the Roshi meant I was not to undo the bonds of the vow I had made to become a Zen monk. And so, with resolution so firm that it gripped my whole frame, I bowed deeply to my teacher and went into the pitch darkness bound for Daitokuji monastery.

Persevering at the Monastery Entrance

When I arrived at the entrance to the monastery I took off my wicker hat, placed it to one side on the dirt floor, crouched down before the wooden step, and called out for admission. In Zen monasteries the entrance area usually has a dirt floor; from there a few steps lead up to wide corridors on either side of the building. Though dozens of monks might be training on the premises, it is as quiet as the grave. Again I loudly called out the traditional greeting, but my voice seemed to be swallowed up in the silent depths.

Then from the innermost part of the building someone demanded, "Who is there?" A senior monk appeared. "Where are you from?" he asked. With my head still bowed down to the floor, I handed him the required documents: my curriculum vitae, my petition to be allowed to train in the monastery, and my pledge that I would give myself to the training even if it cost my life. I begged him to announce my arrival to the master. "Please wait a moment," he said as he withdrew. When the monk returned he told me, "You look too frail for the extremely hard training here. Better go to another monastery." These days I weigh about a hundred fifty pounds, but at that time I was a mere hundred five.

I knew that an aspiring Zen monk is always refused entrance on some excuse, such as "This monastery is already full," or "This monastery is very poor and cannot afford to keep you." These responses are part of a test called *niwazume,* which has precedents in ancient Zen lore. The Indian monk Bodhidharma is considered the Twenty-eighth Partriarch after Shakyamuni and the First Patriarch of Zen. After Bodhidharma arrived in China, Hui-k'o (called Eka in Japanese) begged to be his disciple. Tradition reports that Eka stood day after day waiting for Bodhidharma to respond to him. Even when the falling snow reached up to his knees, he stood firm. Finally, in order to show Bodhidharma the sincerity of his resolve, Eka took the hatchet slung at his waist, hacked off his left arm, and offered it to the master. At last Bodhidharma accepted Eka as his disciple. Later Eka became the Second Patriarch of Zen. This is why even today, nearly fifteen hundred years after Eka's ordeal, the procedure for entering a Zen monastery is so severe. I was well aware of this background, so I took back my rejected documents, crouched by a bench in the corner, and continued to call out fervently for admission. I thought this ritual was a matter of form and did not suspect the real severity of it.

After a while another monk appeared, armed with an oaken staff. "You were refused entrance, and yet you are still here, an eyesore to all. Please get out at once." When I made no move to leave, the monk changed his tone. "Deaf or something?" he shouted, and with blows and kicks he sent me flying out of the gate. When I peered back inside I saw the monk had disappeared again. So I crept back stealthily and took up my position at the bench. This sequence was repeated several times. At the beginning I was able to put up with it because I thought it was a form I must follow. But gradually I started to get angry—they seemed to be laying it on a bit thick against someone who was putting up no resistance. By evening my anger had disappeared, and instead I felt utterly forlorn. I fell to thinking, "What on earth am I doing, crouching in pain in this entrance hall, allowing myself to be treated worse than an old floorcloth? Even though my parents are dead, I still have some relatives in Toyama; I can always go home. I don't have to put up with this!"

I had left Daishuin with considerable resolution for entering Daitokuji. When Zuigan Roshi had said, "This is Nirvana money for the disposal of your corpse," and when he had tied the strings of my sandals, my determination seemed unshakeable. My parting with him had taken place earlier that same day, and yet my resolve had already begun to falter in face of the misery and turmoil which had welled up in me. I was discovering that an individual's strength of will is extremely weak. This point is especially relevant to the young people of today. Until you have subjected yourself to some discipline, you should not put too much faith in your own willpower. When I saw my own will crumbling at the monastery entrance, I suddenly felt I understood the reason for niwazume. As one crouches by the bench on the dirt floor, one's resolve is put to the test time and again.

My niwazume lasted three days. By the end my face was congested with blood. All my teeth felt loose, my eyes felt as though they were popping out of their sockets, and my hips felt as if they had been wrenched out of joint. I had come to Daitokuji on the first of March, and it was bitterly cold that year. All I had on my feet were sodden straw sandals. The cold had risen from my toes to my thighs—my legs had become completely frozen and numb. I think it was an act of real courage to go on and on in this state, pulling myself back from the brink of exhaustion and despair to carry through with my vow to practice Zen. When I was in school, I would sometimes pick a quarrel with someone to show how brave I was. However, fighting with others is not courage; it is behaving like a small dog with a loud bark. Real courage is enduring and holding firm in the face of one's own faint-heartedness. I would not have learned the truth of this had I not been forced to question myself over and over again.

Many thoughts passed through my mind during those three days at the monastery entrance. The interminable hours made me think also of all those who come to practice in a monastery. They are from different backgrounds, with different talents, experiences, and concerns. There would be little likelihood for any effective training in the monastery if each person were to insist on having things run the way that suited him. In the West there is the saying, "New wine must be put in new bottles." I realized that if I intended to pour the new wisdom of enlightenment into my own vessel, I must enter the monastery completely emptied, humble, and compliant. I had to discard all my previous social standing, knowledge, and opinions.

During the evening of the third day the monk on duty came out and said, "As you are still here despite having been scolded and beaten, you show some measure of resolve to practice, so you may come in. However, you are not yet formally admitted, so you had better keep your wits about you." Allowed in at long last, I was taken to a room open to full view, with but a single wall. The sliding doors on the other three sides were open. I put my bunko down and sat in zazen facing the wall, which was all I could see. As anybody might be looking in from the other three sides, I could not relax for a moment. I was given three simple meals a day, and at night I was provided with a sleeping mat and allowed to sleep. I spent five days in that open room, so for a total of eight days I kept asking myself why I was there and what I was trying to do. Time and time again I had to remind myself of the vow I had made to practice, rally my flagging resolve, and repeat that vow. Thus I became a monk at Daitokuji monastery.

After fifteen years of hard Zen training, I received inka from my teacher. I was able to persevere through those long years of practice thanks to what I had learned at the very outset—through experience, not theory. At Daishuin I had been shown the meaning of trust. At the entrance of Daitokuji I had learned the meaning of the courage which has its roots in faith and which remains undaunted whatever resistance is encountered.

Zen master Hakuin identified three essentials of Zen practice, and these apply in many other realms as well: a great root of faith, a great ball of doubt, and a fierce tenacity of purpose. The great root of faith means trusting one's teacher and the tradition he represents. It also means believing in the limitless potentiality that lies within oneself. Though at first glance it would appear that a great ball of doubt is the exact opposite of a great root of faith, it means to be aware at all times of one's own lack of insight and to harbor within oneself a deep distrust of "I." Fierce tenacity of purpose means to have the real courage to continue the practice, whatever the obstacles. Without these three essentials, nothing can be accomplished. I realized the truth of Hakuin's words not by listening to sermons or reading books, but by practical experience. Had I not learned these lessons at Daishuin and the entrance to Daitokuji, I doubt that a half-hearted young man in his twenties would have found the strength to persevere in a Zen monastery. However much society may change, I am convinced that Hakuin's three essentials constitute the cornerstone of all achievement.

People today have lost the feeling of trust in their education and in their daily lives. Especially among younger people it has become acceptable to criticize one's surroundings, to shirk one's responsibilities, and to change one's mind continually. Adults commonly pander to the young. Schoolteachers think it is their job to make their classes as appealing as possible to their pupils, and parents are encouraged to dote on their children and raise them with the least possible constraint. Yet how understanding is the society these children will eventually enter? Far from being a world full of fellow-feeling and mutual consideration, it is a world where everyone is concerned solely with himself. People not only ignore the misfortune of others, they may be secretly pleased by their neighbor's straitened circumstances. As a result, when children pampered by easy-going parents and educated by amiable teachers step into the world as it is, they become confused and despondent. How could it be otherwise, since their upbringing and education have taught them neither self-reliance nor resourcefulness?

Why are you reading this account? If just out of curiosity, you will only have learned about someone who lives in a different world from your own. Rather than discuss satori or the heart of Zen, I have presumed to relate my own experiences as a young monk because I hope readers will find something of practical use, something relevant to their daily lives. I am not especially concerned that Buddhism flourishes or that the Zen school prospers. What I consider most important is that each individual lives a truly fulfilled and contented life, at peace even in the face of death. That is the primary aim of Zen, no matter how foreign its external form may at times appear.

Translated by James Stokes[2]

2. Zen Meditation

by Sheng-Yen

The Chinese term *tso-ch'an* (*zazen* in Japanese) was in use among Buddhist practitioners even before the appearance of the Ch'an (Zen) school. *Tso* literally means "sitting." *Ch'an* is a derivative of the Indian *dhyāna,* which is the yogic practice of attaining a unified mind in meditation. In a broad sense, tso-ch'an refers to any type of meditative practice based on taking the sitting posture. In a more narrow sense, it indicates the methods of meditation that characterize Ch'an/Zen Buddhism.

The following criteria for correct zazen practice have not changed since ancient days. Sit on the floor with the legs crossed either in the full lotus or half lotus position. To make the full lotus, put the right foot on the left thigh, then put the left foot crossed over the right leg onto the right thigh. For the half lotus position only one foot is crossed over onto the thigh of the other; the other foot remains underneath the raised leg.

Though the full or half lotus are the preferred zazen postures, they may be too difficult for some people. One alternative is called the Burmese position. It is similar to the half lotus, except that one foot is crossed over onto the calf, rather than the thigh, of the other leg. Another acceptable position is kneeling, legs together and back erect. In this position, the buttocks can rest on the heels, on a cushion placed between the feet, or on a specially designed bench. If physical problems prevent sitting in any of the above positions, then sitting on a chair is possible as a last resort.

Sitting cross-legged is most conducive to long periods of zazen with effective concentration. But the position you can take may depend on such factors as physical condition, health, and age. You should use a position in which at least twenty minutes of immobile zazen is feasible and reasonably comfortable. However, do not choose the position that requires the least exertion, because good results cannot be attained without the effort to discipline the body-mind. If sitting on the floor, sit on a Japanese-style *zafu* (round meditation cushion) or other improvised cushion, several inches thick. This is partly for comfort, but also because it is easier to maintain an erect spine if the buttocks are slightly raised. Place a larger square pad, such as a Japanese *zabuton,* underneath the cushion. Sit with the buttocks toward the front half of the cushion, the knees resting firmly on the pad.

The spine must be upright. Rather than thrusting your chest forward, make sure your lower back is erect. The chin must be tucked in slightly, without tipping the head down. An upright spine also means a vertical spine; do not lean forward or backward, right or left. Let the shoulders be relaxed and the arms hang loosely. If you have any sensation of shoulders, arms, or hands, there is probably tension in that area. The hands are placed in front of the abdomen, resting on the legs. The open right palm is underneath, and the open left palm rests in the right palm. The thumbs lightly touch to form a closed circle or oval.

The mouth must always be closed. At all times breathe through the nose, not the mouth. The tip of the tongue should be lightly touching the roof of the mouth just behind the front teeth. If you have too much saliva, you can let go of this connection. If you have no saliva at all, you can apply greater pressure with the tip of the tongue. The eyes should be slightly open, gazing downward at a forty-five degree angle. Let the eyes rest without focusing on anything. Closing the eyes may cause drowsiness or visual illusions. However, if your eyes feel very tired you can close them for a short while.

Walking meditation is useful for a change of pace when engaged in prolonged sitting, such as on personal or group retreats. In slow walking, the upper body should be in the same posture as in sitting, though the hands are held differently. The left palm lightly encloses the right hand, which is a loosely formed fist. Joined in this way, the hands should be held in front of the abdomen, forearms parallel to the ground. Focus attention on the bottom of the feet as you walk with measured steps. If walking in an enclosed space, walk in a clockwise direction. Fast walking, another method, is walking energetically without actually running. The main difference in posture is that the arms are now dropped to the sides, swinging naturally. Take short fast steps, keeping the attention on the feet.

Regulating the breath is very simple: just breathe naturally. Do not try to control your breathing. The breath is used as a way to focus or concentrate the mind; that is, regulating the breath and regulating the mind are brought together. The basic method is to count one's breath in a repeating cycle of ten. Through concentration on the simple technique of counting, the mind is less vulnerable to wandering thoughts. Starting with one, mentally (not vocally) count each exhalation until you reach ten, keeping the full attention on the counting. After reaching ten, start over again with one. Do not count during the inhalation, but just keep the mind on the intake of air through the nose. When random thoughts occur while counting, ignore them and continue counting. If wandering thoughts cause you to lose count or go beyond ten, as soon as you become aware of it start over again at one. If you have so many distracting thoughts that keeping count is impossible, you can vary the method—counting backward from ten to one, or counting by twos from two to twenty.

When wandering thoughts are minimal, and you can consistently maintain the count without losing it, you can drop counting and just observe your breath going in and out. Keep your attention at the tip of your nose. Do not try to control the tempo or depth of your breathing; just watch it. When you become aware that you have been interrupted by thoughts, return at once to the practice. Another method of regulating the mind is to focus the attention on the *tan-t'ien* (*tanden* in Japanese), which is a point located just below the navel. The tan-t'ien is not an organ but a center of psychic energy. This method is best employed when breathing has descended naturally to the abdomen. Mentally follow the movements of the tan-t'ien as the abdomen moves in and out naturally with each breath. This method is more energetic than counting or following the breath, and it should be used only after gaining some proficiency in those two techniques.

In zazen it is important that body and mind be relaxed. At times of excessive physical or mental tension, forced zazen can be counter-productive. If you are relaxed, the various sensations that arise are usually beneficial (pain, soreness, itchiness, warmth, coolness, and so on). For example, a pain that arises during relaxed zazen may mean that unconscious tensions are benefiting from the circulation of blood and energy induced by meditation. A longstanding problem may thus be alleviated. On the other hand, if you are very tense while doing zazen and feel pain, the tension itself may be causing the pain. A safe and recommended approach is to limit sitting initially to half an hour, or two half-hour segments, in as relaxed a manner as possible. If the mind is overburdened with outside concerns, it may be better to relieve some of those concerns before sitting. For this and other reasons, it is best to sit early in the morning, before the mind fills with the problems of the day. Sitting times may be increased with experience.

Although the methods of zazen given here are simple and straightforward, it is best to practice them under the guidance of a qualified Zen teacher. Without a teacher, a beginning meditator will not be able to correct his or her mistakes, and these could lead to problems or lack of results. The fruits of correct zazen practice include centeredness, calmness, and clarity.

Sheng-Yen

Traditional Approaches to Zazen

The earliest Chinese translations of Buddhist sutras that described methods for achieving a unified mind (*samādhi*) appeared around the end of the second century A.D. In the beginning of the fifth century, Kumārajīva translated into Chinese several more sutras on the practice of meditation, such as the *Sutra on Zazen and Samādhi* (*Tso-ch'an san-mei ching*). During these early centuries many Chinese monks practiced zazen to achieve samadhi in the Indian manner. During the Sui dynasty (589–617), the T'ien-t'ai master Chih-I wrote two seminal works on meditation. He described zazen in terms of three aspects: regulating the body, the breath, and the mind. He also presented four methods for attaining samadhi: constant sitting; constant walking; half walking, half sitting; and neither walking nor sitting. Thus several centuries before the emergence of the Ch'an school in the seventh century, zazen had already reached a high state of development in China, both as a practice and as a scriptural topic. We also note the close association between zazen and samadhi in Chinese Buddhist practice prior to Ch'an.

What is samadhi? Though Indian tradition defines nine levels of samadhi, each with its own identifying characteristics, a general definition will suffice here. Samadhi is a unified state of mind in which there is no distinction between self and environment, no sense of time or place. This is not a state of no-thought or no-mind, since there is still an awareness of the self experiencing samadhi. Rather, it is a state of one-thought or one-mind. In Ch'an, an important distinction is made between samadhi and enlightenment, as seen in the spiritual path of Shakyamuni Buddha. After years of austere practice as a yogi, Shakyamuni had attained the highest level of samadhi, but he knew that his realization was still incomplete. He sat under the *bodhi* tree, vowing not to get up until he had fully resolved the question of death and rebirth. Only when he became enlightened, after seeing the morning star, did he rise. His experience became the paradigm of zazen practice.

The First Patriarch of Ch'an, the Indian monk Bodhidharma, reached China around A.D. 520 and established himself in Shaolin temple. While the historical facts of Bodhidharma's life are scant, there is little doubt that he was enlightened before arriving in China. Even so, he continued zazen practice. According to legend, Bodhidharma sat facing a wall for nine years, in the same posture used by previous masters to attain samadhi. However, he did not use Hinayana methods (such as visualizing parts of the body), and his goal was different—to attain liberation without necessarily going through samadhi. Bodhidharma's great contribution to Ch'an was his insistence on directly experiencing Buddha-nature through zazen.

The Fourth Patriarch, Tao-hsin (580–651), similarly stressed the importance of zazen. For the novice, he advocated contemplation of the five aggregates of human existence: corporeality, feeling, perception, mental formation, and consciousness. In his *Methods for Entering the Path and Calming the Mind* (*Ju-tao an-hsin yao fang-pien men*), Tao-hsin quoted an earlier text:

> One should contemplate the five aggregates as originally empty, quiescent, non-arising, non-perishing, equal, and without differentiation. Constantly thus practicing, day or night, whether sitting, walking, standing, or lying down, one finally reaches an inconceivable state without any obstruction or form. This is called the Samadhi of One Act.

Tao-hsin's disciple, the Fifth Patriarch Hung-jen (600–674), is said to have foregone sleep to meditate all night. In his essay "Treatise on the Essentials of Cultivating the Mind" (*Hsiu-hsin yao lun*) he taught, "When the mind is placed at one point, there is nothing that cannot be attained." The one-pointedness to which he referred was not samadhi, but one's original or true mind.

The Sixth Patriarch Hui-neng (638–713) offered some novel

formulations of zazen. In his *Platform Sutra* (*Liu-tsu t'an ching*), he says that if one were to stay free from attachment to any mental or physical realms and to refrain from discriminating, neither thoughts nor mind would arise. This is the true "sitting" of Ch'an. Here the term "sitting" is not limited to physical sitting but refers to a practice where the mind is not influenced or disturbed by anything that arises, internally or in the environment. For Hui-neng, the direct experience of Self-nature, the seeing of one's own unmoving Buddha-nature, is called "Ch'an." One could say that true sitting is the method, Ch'an the result. Yet since Ch'an is sudden enlightenment, when it occurs it is simultaneous with zazen. Hui-neng was critical of certain attitudes in practice which did not conform to his criteria of the true zazen that leads to Ch'an. Such "outer path" approaches to sitting are illustrated in the following two anecdotes.

The first story involves a disciple of Hui-neng, Nan-yüeh Huai-jang (677–744). Huai-jang observed a monk named Ma-tsu (709–788), who had a habit of doing zazen all day long. Realizing this was no ordinary monk, Huai-jang asked Ma-tsu, "Why are you constantly doing zazen?" Ma-tsu answered, "To attain buddhahood." Huai-jang picked up a brick and started rubbing it vigorously. After a while Ma-tsu asked, "What are you doing?" Huai-jang said, "I'm making a mirror from this brick." Ma-tsu said, "That's absurd. You can't make a mirror from a brick." Huai-jang said, "Indeed. And how is it possible to become a buddha by doing zazen?" Thereupon Ma-tsu asked, "What should I do?" Huai-jang said, "When the ox won't pull the cart, do you beat the cart or the ox?" Ma-tsu did not know how to reply. So Huai-jang said, "Are you doing zazen to attain Ch'an or to become a buddha? If it's Ch'an, Ch'an is neither sitting nor lying down; if it's buddhahood, Buddha has no form. Since the Dharma has no abiding form, there should be no grasping, no rejection. Your attachment to sitting prevents you from realizing buddhahood, and it kills Buddha besides." Ma-tsu became a disciple of Huai-jang and eventually a great master himself.

This story teaches that true zazen is not just a matter of sitting, however dedicated or perfected. To do zazen with Ma-tsu's original understanding will bring some benefits. But it is impossible to attain Ch'an simply by perfecting the external form of zazen. Self-nature is to be found in what Huai-jang called the "mind-ground," not in the realm of form. Later Ma-tsu reiterated this point in his concept of "ordinary mind" (*p'ing-ch'ang*). One sense of this expression is a mind that is involved in the ordinary world, moving as usual but not clinging to anything. Another sense comes from the root meanings of *p'ing* and *ch'ang,* which suggest a mind that is "level" and "constant," or in a state of constant equanimity. In either sense, there is no attachment.

The second "outer path" anecdote also involves disciples of Hui-neng. When Shih-t'ou Hsi-ch'ien (700–790) was a young monk, he approached the dying Hui-neng and asked, "Master, after you pass away, what should I do?" Hui-neng said, "You should go to Hsing-ssu." Shih-t'ou understood him to say *"hsun-ssu,"* which means "seek thoughts." So he assumed that the master told him to practice watching his thoughts, a known method of meditation. Shih-t'ou was unaware that there was another disciple of Hui-neng by the name of Ch'ing-yuan Hsing-ssu (d. 740). After Hui-neng died, Shih-t'ou sought isolated places and spent his time there in zazen, neglecting all else. An elder monk in the assembly saw this and said, "What are you doing here in empty sitting?" Shih-t'ou replied, "I am only following my master's instructions. He told me to watch my thoughts." The elder said, "You should realize you have a senior Dharma brother whose name is Hsing-ssu. Why don't you go study with him?"

Indeed, the zazen which consists of sitting in a quiet place, immersed in tranquility, is widely practiced. This kind of meditation, which Shih-t'ou used until he learned of his error, was also criticized by Hui-neng in the *Transmission of the Lamp* (*Ching-te ch'uan teng lu*):

> If you just hold the mind and contemplate silently, this is a disease and not Ch'an. How does constantly sitting, restraining your body, actualize the principle (of attaining enlightenment)?

Peaceful zazen can enhance mental and physical health and even lead to samadhi, but "empty sitting" is ultimately an obstacle to genuine realization.

Though both of these anecdotes criticize certain approaches toward zazen practice, the masters were never critical of zazen itself, which is necessary for progress in Ch'an. All the great masters practiced zazen, and most of them continued to sit intensely even after becoming enlightened. The descriptions of the earliest Ch'an monasteries in the *Biographies of Eminent Monks* (*Kao-seng chuan*) confirm that monks were supposed to spend most of their time in zazen.

Silent Illumination and Koan Practice

Earlier we noted that zazen most precisely refers to the means developed by the Ch'an masters to attain enlightenment. The two principal paths of Ch'an which have come down to us are the method of "silent illumination" and the method of the *kōan* (*kung-an* in Chinese).

The practice of silent illumination may be traced back at least as far as Bodhidharma. In his (attributed) treatise *The Two Entries and the Four Practices* (*Ehr ju ssu hsing lun*), he states:

> Leaving behind the false, return to the true: make no discrimination of self and others. In contemplation one is stable and unmoving, like a wall.

Shih-shuang Ch'ing-chu (805–888) lived on a mountain called Shih-shuang for twenty years. His disciples just sat continually, even sleeping in this upright position. In their stillness they looked like so many dead tree stumps, and they were called "the dry-wood Sangha." Shih-shuang had two famous phrases of advice. One was: "To sit Ch'an, fix your mind on one thought for ten thousand years." The other was: "Become like cold ashes or dry wood."

The Sung dynasty master Hung-chih Cheng-chüeh (1091–1157), the best-known advocate of silent illumination, studied with a master called K'u-mu ("Dry-wood"), whose body resembled a block of wood when he sat. Hung-chih describes "silent sitting" as follows:

> Your body sits silently; your mind is quiescent, unmoving. This is genuine effort in practice. Body and mind are at complete rest. The mouth is so still that moss grows around it. Grass sprouts from the tongue. Do this without cease, cleansing the mind until it gains the clarity of an autumn pool and the brightness of the moon illuminating the evening sky. . . . In this silent sitting, whatever realms may appear the mind remains very clear in all details, with everything in its own original place. The mind stays on one thought for ten thousand years, yet does not dwell on any forms, inside or outside.

Silent illumination differs from outer path zazen, which generates a samadhi that lacks wisdom. By itself samadhi is silent but not illuminating. In silent illumination the mind is not fixed in samadhi but dwells in a bright state of illumination, which the meditator continually works to maintain. Although there are no thoughts, the mind is still very clear and aware. If such a nonattached state of mind can be maintained throughout one's daily life, that is true Ch'an.

In Japanese Zen the type of zazen called *shikantaza* ("just sitting") is quite similar to silent illumination. It was introduced in Japan by Master Dōgen (1200–1253) after his return from China. In his work *Principles of Zazen for Everyone* (*Fukanzazengi*), Dōgen writes:

> You should therefore cease from practice based on intellectual understanding, pursuing words and following after speech, and

learn the backward step that turns your light inwardly to illuminate yourself. Body and mind of themselves will drop away, and your original face will manifest.

Koan practice is taken up by Roshis Kapleau and Eido in the next two chapters, so the treatment here will be brief. A koan is an account of an incident between a master and one or more disciples which involves an understanding or experience of enlightened mind. A koan usually, but not always, involves dialogue. When the original incident is remembered and recorded, it becomes a "public case," which is the literal meaning of koan. Often what makes the incident worth recording is that the disciple's mind, if only for an instant, transcends attachment and logic, and he catches a glimpse of emptiness or Buddha-nature. At that moment there is a "transmission" of Mind between master and disciple. Once, after the Buddha gave a sermon to his senior disciples, he picked up a flower and silently held it up before the assembly. All the monks except one were mystified. Mahakasyapa alone knew the Buddha's meaning; he smiled, saying nothing. Thus the Buddha transmitted to Mahakasyapa the wordless doctrine of Mind. Although this incident preceded the rise of Ch'an by over a thousand years, it exemplifies the spirit of koans.

The earliest koans were spontaneous incidents that arose naturally in the context of practice. During the Sung dynasty (960–1279), Ch'an masters began using these "public cases" as a method of meditation for their disciples. In attempting to plumb the meaning of a koan, one has to abandon knowledge, experience, and reasoning, since the answer is not susceptible to these methods. The student must find the answer by "becoming one" with the koan. Only when there is nothing left in the mind but the koan is awakening possible.

Closely related to the koan is the *hua-t'ou* (literally "head of a thought"), a question that the meditator inwardly asks himself. "What is Mu?" or "Who am I?" are two good examples. As with the koan, the answer is not resolvable through reasoning. The meditator devotes his full attention to asking himself the hua-t'ou, over and over. His objective is to probe into the source of the question, that is, the state of mind that existed before the question became a thought.

Koans and hua-t'ous are both methods of *ts'an Ch'an*, "investigating Ch'an." Because the Buddha sometimes used a question-and-answer format to deepen the understanding of his disciples, the word *ts'an* is also applicable to the Buddha's teaching methods. Another instance of ts'an Ch'an is the practice of making the rounds to accomplished masters in order to engage them in dialogue. Sometimes the practitioner has reached an impasse in his investigation, and he needs some "turning words" from a master to give him the impetus for a breakthrough. Advanced practitioners also visited masters in order to assess their own understanding of Ch'an or certify their own attainment. Koans and hua-t'ous were well-suited to these situations. Any interchange between master and disciple can be an opportunity for a live, spontaneous koan or hua-t'ou; these practices are not limited to sayings and questions from the historical record.

Another way in which koans and hua-t'ous are related is that a hua-t'ou can give rise to a koan, and vice versa. For example, the question "If all the myriad things in the universe return to the One, to what does the One return?" was originally a hua-t'ou. When a student asked Master Chao-chou this same question, he answered, "When I was in Ch'ing Province I had one hempen shirt made weighing seven pounds." This exchange became an important koan. Conversely, a key phrase in a koan frequently serves as the source for a hua-t'ou. Thus "What is Mu?" is derived from the koan "Does a dog have Buddha-nature?"

P'ang Yün (d. 808), a lay disciple of Ma-tsu, resolved to follow the Path. He threw his wealth into the river and became a basket weaver. While plying his trade one day, he met a monk begging for alms. Giving the monk some money, P'ang asked him, "What is the meaning of giving alms?" The monk said, "I don't know. What is the meaning of giving alms?" And P'ang replied, "Very few people have heard about it." The monk said, "I don't understand." P'ang then asked, "Who is it that doesn't understand?" This incident became a koan that gave birth to a whole series of hua-t'ous of the "who" type. Some variations on it are: "Who is reciting Buddha's name?" "Who is investigating Ch'an?" "Who is dragging this corpse?" and so on.

Zazen and Enlightenment

The records of the Ch'an sect, including the *Transmission of the Lamp* and the koan collections, do not refer to zazen practice very often. It was commonly understood that by the time practitioners began to "investigate Ch'an," they already had a good foundation in zazen. Beginners without much zazen experience may get some use out of the constant (silent) repetition of a koan or hua-t'ou, but this will only be like reciting a *mantra.* Without the ability to bring the mind to a deep quiescent state, it is virtually impossible to experience Self-nature through work on a koan. Thus Ta-hui Tsung-kao (1089–1163), one of the greatest advocates of koan practice, consistently maintained that zazen was necessary to settle the wandering mind.

If a student's mind has become stable through zazen, the application of the koan may generate the Great Doubt. This doubt is not the ordinary doubt that questions the truth of an assertion. It refers to the practitioner's deeply questioning state of mind which results from investigating the koan. In fact, the resolution of the koan hinges on the nurturing of the Great Doubt. Because the meditator cannot answer his question by logic, he must continually return to the question itself, and this process clears the mind of everything except the Great Doubt. The "doubt mass" that accumulates can disappear in one of two ways. Due to lack of concentration or energy, the meditator may not be able to sustain the doubt, and it will dissipate. But if he persists until his doubt is like a "hot ball of iron stuck in his throat," the doubt mass will burst apart in an explosion.

If that explosion has enough energy, it is possible that the student will become enlightened. A master is needed to confirm the experience since the student, with rare exceptions, cannot do that himself. Even as great a figure as Ta-hui did not penetrate sufficiently on his first experience. His master Yuan-wu K'o-ch'in (1063–1135) told him, "You have died, but you haven't come back to life." Ta-hui was confirmed on his second enlightenment experience. Without the guidance of a genuine master such as Yuan-wu, Ta-hui may have settled unwittingly for a partial realization.

In the early twelfth century, Ch'ang-lu Tsung-tse wrote the *Manual of Zazen* (*Tso-ch'an i*). He insisted that a person who has experienced Buddha-nature should continue to practice zazen. Then one can become like a dragon who gains the water, or a tiger who enters the mountains. A dragon gaining the water returns to his ancestral home, free to dive as deep as he wishes. A tiger entering the mountains has no opposition; he may ascend the heights and roam at will. Thus Zen teaches that zazen after enlightenment enhances and deepens one's realization.

Yüeh-shan Wei-yen (745–828), an enlightened monk, was doing zazen. His master Shih-t'ou asked him, "What are you doing zazen for?" Yüeh-shan answered, "Not for anything." "That means you are sitting idly," said Shih-t'ou. Yüeh-shan countered, "If this is idle sitting, then that would be for something." The master then said, "What is it that is not for anything?" The monk answered, "A thousand sages won't know." On the one hand, we say that persons who have had realization should continue to do zazen to enhance their enlightenment. On the other hand, we say the enlightened person sits without purpose. For the practitioner whose enlightenment is not deep, further zazen is necessary to deepen it; for one who is deeply enlightened, zazen is just part of daily life. Here we recall Hui-neng's conception of true zazen: it is not limited to sitting, and the mind does not abide in anything. The ultimate zazen is no zazen.

3. The Private Encounter with the Master

By Philip Kapleau

In the thirty-five years since Dr. D. T. Suzuki introduced an intellectually-oriented Zen to the West—the inevitable first step—the literature of Zen has ballooned, now filling many library shelves. Yet this vast literary production contains few volumes on actual Zen training. Rarely examined is one crucial aspect of the training process—*dokusan* ("going alone"), the eyeball-to-eyeball encounter with the master (*rōshi*) in the privacy of his teaching room. My book *The Three Pillars of Zen,* first published in 1965, sought to fill this lacuna by describing my own and other practitioners' experiences in dokusan. Now, after some twenty years as a teacher, I am in a position to speak about this encounter from a different perspective—to clarify its function and to tell what lies behind a teacher's words and actions.

The private encounter with the Zen master is one of the three pillars on which Zen training rests; the other two are meditation (*zazen*) and the master's commentary (*teishō*). No English word conveys the precise meaning and spirit of dokusan, only because no such mode of spiritual training has existed in our own culture until recent times. The private encounter is not an interview in which a would-be student answers questions about himself, explains why he wants to practice Zen, and perhaps asks a variety of questions unrelated to practice. Nor is it a simple, friendly meeting. Neither does it involve a discussion of Buddhist doctrine in the manner of the classroom. Still less is it a counseling session during which a student may seek advice on matters affecting personal relationships. In dokusan the teacher probes the student's understanding and realization, if any, and gives him pointers for future practice. With a more advanced student the "testing" is more active, as the teacher tries to evoke a demonstration of the student's understanding, not unlike the insertion of an irritant into an oyster to cause it to produce a pearl.

Individual instruction is a teaching method in Buddhism that is said to go back to the time of the Buddha, when monks assembled in caves for intensive training during the three-month rainy season. Later in China a more open form of encounter between teacher and students developed. In Japan, and in Korea too, the Zen masters added a new and vigorous dimension in which dokusan became less a matter of didactic instruction and more a form of testing. It is this style that is most common in Zen centers in the West today, with modifications that reflect our own cultural and psychological characteristics. Before discussing these inner aspects, let me describe some of dokusan's outer, formal procedures.

Upon entering the roshi's room the student, with hands palm to palm, first makes a standing bow and then proceeds to a mat in front of the roshi. There he or she prostrates once as a sign of respect and humility. Although prostration is traditional among Asians, I do not insist upon it. Eventually most students, even those in whom such a gesture raises shackles of resistance at first, come to see its value as a "horizontalizing of the mast of ego," and they perform it willingly.

Dokusan is announced in the *zendō* (meditation hall) with a clanging of the roshi's handbell. Those who wish to go before him—and this is optional—quickly leave their seats in the zendo in order to get a place in the waiting line. They proceed to mats lined up before a small bell suspended from a wooden frame. When the roshi rings his handbell, the student at the head of the line strikes the bell in front of him twice with a padded wooden mallet and then enters the roshi's chamber. The whole line then moves up one place. When the waiting sitters have all seen the roshi, the monitors in the zendo signal the next group to line up. And so on until all who wish private instruction have had it.

These procedures are more than ceremonial. Besides preserving a sense of order, they aid the roshi in determining the mind state of the student. Has he or she hit the bell firmly or with a glancing blow? Is the striking hasty or sluggish? Has the bell been struck too loudly or too softly, or is one strike noisier or quieter than the other? In short, *how* the bell is struck tells the roshi, who can hear the sound in his room, whether the student is a beginner or a more advanced student and what the condition of his or her mind is.

How long does an individual's meeting with the roshi take? It varies. Sometimes it may be only a minute or two, at other times as long as fifteen minutes or half an hour. The length is determined not by any arbitrary time limit but by the needs of the student. Much depends, too, on whether the meeting with the roshi is the student's first, which is usually lengthy, or whether the student is working on a first koan or a subsequent koan. During intensive meditation sessions (*sesshin*), there may be as many as forty or fifty participants. Since most of them want to avail themselves of every opportunity for private instruction, the roshi cannot in fairness entertain questions extraneous to a student's practice without penalizing the others waiting their turn. Dokusan is not the proper time to bring up personal matters or raise theoretical questions.

Of the three facets of Zen training mentioned above (zazen, the roshi's commentary, and dokusan), dokusan offers the greatest opportunity for personal growth and spiritual awakening. Thus it is held three times a day during a seven-day sesshin, while the commentary is given only once daily. Although the three facets are not unrelated, they have different functions and purposes.

In zazen, the practice of looking into one's own mind, the student is on his own as he seeks to gain control over his wayward thoughts. As he faces a wall or divider, symbolic of his stubborn ego, neither the master nor anyone else can substitute for him. In this solitary voyage into the vast hidden world of mind, all of one's inner resources must be brought to bear by oneself on oneself. This process I have described previously as:

> a lonely trek through winding canyons of shame and fear, across deserts of ecstatic visions and tormenting phantasms, around volcanoes of oozing ego, and through jungles of folly and delusion in a ceaseless struggle to gain that oneness and emptiness of body and mind which ultimately lead to the lightning-and-thunder discovery that the universe and oneself are not remote and apart but an intimate, palpitating whole.[1]

In the commentary the roshi takes center stage for a solo performance. His talk of approximately an hour facing the Buddha altar is less a sermon on Buddhist doctrine or a philosophical discourse on the nature of ultimate reality than a vivid, straight-from-the-gut *demonstration* of reality itself. Charged with all the energy of his liberated mind, his talk inspires, instructs, and points the way to future effort.

In the private encounter the student comes on stage in a contrapuntal duet with the teacher. Often dreaded if he is a beginner yet eagerly sought by him if he is an advanced student, dokusan is his long-awaited confrontation with the teacher, his time to shine or simply to make himself like a sponge, soaking up the truth the teacher is thrusting before him. The juxtaposition of their postures reinforces the idea of confrontation (in the mild sense of the word), for they face each other with no more than two feet separating them. The teacher usually sits in the lotus posture on a round cushion placed on a square mat, while the student kneels on a mat, back erect, perhaps with a cushion between his buttocks and heels. Zen rejects asceticism, and the teacher does not insist on a prescribed position that may turn out to be painful for the student. With the back straight and the body-mind's center of gravity resting in the region two inches below the navel (the *tanden*), the student's mind is denuded of random thoughts. Thus he can more easily and quickly respond with his total being and not simply from the head.

The Master-Disciple Relationship in Zen

While everyone is free to practice zazen and listen to the roshi's commentary, the essential nature of dokusan is the forming of a karmic bond between the roshi and a student, the significance of which is deep in Buddhism. So the personal encounter is not something to be taken lightly. Since what passes between the roshi and the student concerns matters of a deep and ultimate nature, only the truth must be spoken between them. For these reasons, many centers have a rule that one must become a personal student of the roshi before receiving private instruction from him. And because the relationship is a karmic one, it implies that the student will not lightly seek another teacher.

Let me clarify the differences between the master-disciple relationship (in a Zen context) and the teacher-student relationship (in a secular setting). In the ideal teacher-student relationship the student respects the teacher as the possessor of a certain body of knowledge or of a skill that the student would like to acquire, while the teacher values the student for his eagerness and his ability to absorb this knowledge. Their relationship is largely impersonal and limited; what sustains it is their common interest in a particular study. The master-disciple relationship of Zen is deeper and more personal because it is grounded in a karmic affinity. What moves the disciple in the direction of the master is not the master's knowledge but his compassion, enlightened wisdom, character, and warm personality—traits born of long discipline and training. The disciple senses that it is through these qualities that he will be able to complete himself and eventually come to full awakening.[2] At its highest level the relationship between master and disciple may even be stronger than the link between parent and child. In this bond the master assumes responsibility for the disciple's spiritual development, while the disciple undertakes responsibility for the master's economic and general well-being.

The direction a student's meeting with the roshi takes depends primarily on his aspiration. Does he want to train in Zen only to eradicate mental confusion, frustrations, or the bodily pains that usually spring from them? Is his interest in Zen primarily philosophical or literary? Or is his motivation simply to cultivate *samādhi* power for the practice of a martial art? All those worthwhile objectives can be accomplished through zazen properly practiced. From the standpoint of Zen Buddhism, however, they constitute low levels of aspiration. Only if one aspires to enlightenment itself is one's aspiration truly spiritual.

At a new student's first appearance before me I will question him carefully about his aspiration. If it is awakening, does he have the conviction that he can realize it? Does he have the determination to do so? And is he willing to dedicate himself to achieving it? If his answer to each of these questions is an unequivocal "Yes," he is usually assigned a koan, one with which he has an affinity. However, koans are not assigned to a student with no previous experience of zazen. It is desirable that he first engage in breath exercises to gain control over his unruly thoughts. One must acquire what in Zen is called a "seat," the ability to deal calmly with the vicissitudes of one's life. Until one reaches this point, it is futile to try to grapple with a koan. If koan practice is attempted without adequate preparation, the student will quickly become frustrated or bored and give up on the koan and often on Zen itself.

A Zen student in training is constantly being tested, but in this one-to-one encounter the teacher utilizes specific modes of testing, all of which have different purposes. One kind, for example, involves a student who insists he has had an awakening and asks to be tested. "I've had an enlightenment experience. Please test me," he demands of the teacher. Although such an assertion already has a "smell" to it, it cannot safely be ignored. One who has had a valid awakening, even if shallow, does not say, "*I* am enlightened." Nor is enlightenment an *experience* to be grasped among other experiences; it is the ground of all experiences. The teacher will usually comply with a request for testing; otherwise a student may believe he is enlightened when he is not.

If it is common to believe mistakenly that one is enlightened, it can also happen that one has become enlightened and be unaware of it. That is why Dōgen could say, "Do not think you will necessarily be aware of your own enlightenment." There may be understanding on a subconscious level that has not yet found its way into consciousness. So this is another reason why testing is vital.

What sort of testing questions does a teacher ask to establish whether a student has had a genuine awakening? Here are some I myself use:

"Where did you come from when you were born and where will you go when you die?"

"Are you in the universe or is the universe in you?"

"Why is this called a hand (extending hand)?"

"If you had to die right now, what would you do?"

A faltering, uncertain reply or even a simple "I think" can vitiate an entire answer. To be acceptable, the student's response must be spontaneous and sure; understanding must radiate from the eyes and body as well as from the mouth.

Sometimes a student who fails to give satisfactory responses to these questions will protest, "You're asking me Zen questions and I don't know enough about Zen to answer them. But I know I've become enlightened." With such a student I will say, "All right, tell me what happened." He may reply, "I felt as though everything disappeared and I was the only one in the universe." Such a statement can be persuasive if it carries conviction and is accompanied by telltale signs of transformation, but only testing can verify it. When asked "Who is it that knows he is the only one?" few can respond meaningfully. Where there is a deep penetration into truth, most people experience tears of joy. If not simply an emotional reaction, that response may eliminate the need for testing. Yet a student may easily deceive himself or herself. Certain blissful states, hallucinations, the oceanic feeling of oneness, trances, or the sudden cessation of thought—all of which can induce tears of elation and gratitude in one with a strong emotional nature—can be confused with enlightenment.

Testing is vital because there is a fine line between a profound intellectual awareness (based on an experience of insight) and a genuine awakening. In ordinary awakening one may barely open one's eyes, half asleep in a twilight zone, or one may open one's eyes fully and jump out of bed. With *kenshō,* seeing into one's nature, one may see dimly or with great clarity; the gradations are many and subtle.

Another mode of testing is suddenly to jar a student physically or verbally when I sense his mind is ripe, in a state of absolute emptiness. Before I can determine that, however, I scan him carefully with my inner eye as he negotiates the rather long distance to the mat in front of me. Is he rigid and tense, or wobbly and tentative? Are his shoulders drooping or is he walking erect? Most important, what is the condition of his mind? If his head is bent forward and his body stiff and unsteady, the chances are his thoughts are chasing each other like a pack of monkeys stung by a swarm of bees. But if he is in a samadhi state, he will be walking as though not walking.

Again, as he sits in front of me I watch his face intently, especially the eyes. I don't think, "Should I test him, and if so, what kind of procedures should I use?" I must size him up in a split second and intuitively, unthinkingly, apply the incendiary that may ignite the dried tinder of his mind into the flames of self-transcendence. In this type of testing the roshi is like a hen, sensing the precise moment to peck at the egg to liberate the chick from its shell.

In a sesshin a student may give satisfactory responses to the testing questions early on and be unable to answer more than one or two of the same questions at a later time. Or the reverse may happen. Until the third day of a seven-day sesshin, when the energy is still building up, very little can be accomplished by testing in any event. After the third day, however, when the participants are buoyed and sustained by the samadhi power that has accumulated, they may suddenly find themselves able to respond to questions that heretofore baffled them. The human mind is extraordinarily subtle and complex, and there are no precise criteria by which to measure or anticipate its responses. Moreover, we know that the subconscious mind registers and preserves past impressions and experiences that have bypassed the conscious mind. In fact, Zen training can be called a process of bringing into consciousness what was formerly hidden in the subconscious mind. For these reasons a teacher will put the same testing questions to a student early in the sesshin and at a later time, varying the pace, to be certain the student's experiential understanding is real and unshakeable.

Let me illustrate further dimensions of the master-disciple encounter by citing two episodes from the traditional lore of Zen. A clever monk approached the great Zen master Chao-chou and asked, "If all the myriad things in the universe return to the One, to what does the One return?" Very likely the questioner was referring to a passage in the *Gandavyūha Sutra* that says, "All things of the three realms are reduced to the One Mind." The monk's question is like asking "If everything returns to God, where does God return to?" or "What was God doing before he created the world?" When St. Augustine was asked this latter question he quipped, "Creating a hell for the person who asked the question!" That was clever, but had Augustine said it in dokusan he would have been instantly rung out.

To understand why, one needs to savor Chao-chou's response: "When I was in Ch'ing Province I had one hempen shirt made weighing seven pounds." What a seemingly irrelevant reply! But Chao-chou is actually right on target. Obviously the monk is trying to twist the lion's tail, to get Chao-chou to say something like "Emptiness" or "Nothingness," but the master avoids the trap and gives the monk a faultless demonstration of the truth of Zen. Philosophically the question is unanswerable, of course, as Chao-chou and the monk both know. By responding as he does the master not only avoids a meaningless abstraction, he also brings the questioner down to earth, to the concrete and the real, where Zen operates. What could be more real than this seven-pound hempen shirt that can be touched, worn, and experienced through direct contact? Notice, too, how Chao-chou equates oneness with the seven-pound shirt. "All myriad things" are in fact this one, this shirt: one equals seven, seven equals one, one equals all. Try to elaborate oneness, though, and you fall into concepts and abstractions. But fondle the shirt, wear it—become one with it—and you know it directly, concretely, intimately. Ultimate truth can be grasped only through direct experience, not by abstract thought.

This fact is dramatically illustrated in a second encounter, from a well-known koan in the *Gateless Barrier.* The flashpoint that touched off a conflagration in the monk's mind was, appropriately enough, the master's lighting a candle and then suddenly blowing it out. This climax had been preceded by a long discussion on the *Diamond Sutra* between Lung-tan, the master, and Te-shan, a scholar-monk. We can only speculate about the content of their talk, for the koan does not say. But since Te-shan was considered an authority on this scripture, lecturing widely on it, we can presume he questioned the master about it at great length and received the sort of responses that left him suspended in midair. When Lung-tan finally said, "It is getting late, you had better leave," Te-shan's mind was emptied of all the concepts he had been harboring. Peering out, he said, "It's dark outside." Thereupon the master lit a candle and handed it to him. As Te-shan went to take it, Lung-tan suddenly blew it out. With that Te-shan was enlightened.

What prompted the master to blow out the candle? Was it the sudden eruption into his conscious mind of Lao-tzu's observation, "When darkness is at its darkest that is the beginning of all light"? Did he intuitively sense that Te-shan was in a state of absorption to the point of self-forgetfulness, needing only a jolt to precipitate his mind into Self-awareness? His act was literally a "shot in the dark" that struck home.

Dokusan and Koan Training

We now need to consider in some detail a vital aspect of the private encounter—namely, how the roshi deals with students who are investigating koans. This will be done by examining five principal concerns—most of which focus on sesshin, dokusan, or koans—that Zen students and others have expressed over the years. Though some of these objections arise from a limited knowledge of Zen training, they often contain a kernel of truth. Undeniably, the pressures of a seven-day sesshin are intense, especially when keyed to koans and the probing style of dokusan, and the system may have its drawbacks. But my experience as a teacher has convinced me that the advantages of strict sesshin training, with koans and dokusan, far outweigh the disadvantages.

Objection A: Koans Are Grasped Superficially

"Students these days go through whole books of koans (such as the *Gateless Barrier* and the *Blue Cliff Record*) in a superficial manner, in what amounts to assembly-line fashion, without deeply penetrating any of the koans. Contemporary roshis, themselves the product of this "once-over-lightly" system transmitted by their teachers, apply the same low standards to their own students, passing those who have merely tasted but not fully digested a koan. This insidious process begins with the initial breakthrough koan."

Reply

To begin with, it must be recognized that the practice of passing a student who has not fully penetrated his or her koan is a calculated one and not the outcome of ignorance or a "one-more-notch-in-the-belt" complex. In former times, when students had more zeal and ardor, teachers would not sanction a student's enlightenment unless his penetration into the world of oneness (or emptiness or *Mu*) went to the very bottom. Today the distractions and insatiable demands of our complex, technological society, as well as the stresses of coping with rapid change, make such high standards virtually impossible to achieve. How many students nowadays will persist in their training for at least fifteen or twenty years—and hard training at that—until they have had deep awakening? How many contemporary Zen followers could even dream of vowing, as Gautama Buddha and the masters of old did, "Though only my skin, sinews, and bones remain and my blood and flesh dry up and wither away, yet never from this seat will I stir until I have attained full enlightenment"? That kind of determination is too rare these days for a teacher to set his training standards by it. Americans are also handicapped in another way. We are a people impatient for a speedy outcome in whatever we undertake. The "quick fix" is the hallmark of our social, political, economic, and even religious life. If a particular course of action does not bring a quick solution, we soon tire of it and seek faster results elsewhere.

My teacher Yasutani Hakuun Roshi used to say that koans are like offering a tired child sweets to induce him to walk on. This simple statement, however, does not reveal why koans are such a lure to Zen practitioners. In seeking to *demonstrate* the spirit of the masters, as demanded by the koans, the student can relate to the koan's protagonists as flesh-and-blood human beings. A student working on koans has a front-row seat to an ongoing drama in which he is both observer and participant. After several years of zazen focused on breath practices, he is now challenged by the koans to use his mind actively but not analytically. Intellect must transcend itself, entering a wholly new realm in which the unitive mind, the creative intuition, is brought into play. The one-to-one relationship with the roshi enables the student to grasp the Mahayana Buddhist teachings embodied in the koans in the most direct manner possible. And it affords an unparalleled opportunity to experience intimately the spirit and personality of the teacher.

Of course, none of these circumstances imply that masters should pass students who have not penetrated their koans even partially. This point applies to a first koan as well as subsequent ones. With respect to a first koan, the line is often obscure between the darkness before insight and the glimmer of light radiating from a small penetration. Yet an experienced roshi, as we have seen, has many resources at his command by which to test students to be sure that a purported kensho is real. Should a roshi become lax, however, and sanction a student to go on to subsequent koans when the student has not caught even a glimpse of his true nature, the end result is frustration for both of them. For the roshi it is a constant struggle to keep such a student's head above water as the latter flounders helplessly in a sea of koans. Nor is the roshi in less of a predicament if he passes a student who has *barely* opened his Zen eye, for then he may have to extend him a helping hand at every turn as he wallows through the classic koan collections. In some cases, the roshi may find himself in the unenviable position of having to send a student back to the starting line, to Mu or another initial koan. For these reasons a wise roshi will prefer to err on the side of caution.

Generally speaking, a koan brings about awakening more quickly than other types of practice because it provides a tool for focusing one's efforts. The value of even a meager initial insight is that a student who has caught a glimpse of his essential nature is encouraged to persist in his training. Even a small kensho brings greater energy, equanimity, and light into one's life. Attaining kensho quickly through a koan is like vigorously shaking a tree to bring down unripe fruit. Just as green fruit cannot be eaten, so a tiny penetration will not radically transform one's life. But Zen training does not stop with a kensho experience, shallow or deep. Ripening takes place through work on subsequent koans.

No experienced teacher would say to a student who has caught merely a glimpse of his essential nature, "You are enlightened," for such a pat on the back could reinvigorate an ego which has been only temporarily banished from its dominant position in the mind. Besides, until one has integrated this vision into one's life and is able to live by it, one cannot truly be called enlightened. Often the teacher describes to the student the extent and significance of his awakening in terms of the Ten Oxherding pictures, which depict the developing stages of enlightenment, or simply by using some objects at hand. I myself usually point to the square mat in front of me on which the student is sitting and say, "Let us suppose this mat is the world of enlightenment and that the carpet is the unenlightened world. Actually they are not two, but for purposes of comparison let us say they are. From the carpet you have gotten on to the extreme right-hand corner of the mat. There is a qualitative difference between being on the carpet and reaching the mat, even just the corner. Now, a deep penetration would be here," and I point halfway across the mat, "and full enlightenment might be here at the extreme left-hand side of the mat. With subsequent koans you will begin to work your way across the mat."

Then I add: "I must also emphasize that you have not yet fully penetrated your initial koan, as must be apparent to you." I take my baton and say, "The upper side of this stick represents your practice on subsequent koans, and the underside stands for your continuing efforts with Mu. Every time you pass a subsequent koan you reaffirm the world of oneness; that is, you see the world of Mu, beyond the dichotomy of subject and object, more clearly. As a result you will be able to deal with subsequent koans more surely. So the two practices are mutually reinforcing. Through subsequent koans your initial breakthrough can be enlarged and your inner vision expanded."

Passing a first koan is like finally taking hold of the bottom rung of a ladder from the floor of a deep pit into which you have fallen. To grasp this rung after trying for a long time gives you confidence that you can climb the rest of the rungs and escape to freedom. I never cease to marvel at the upsurge in mental and physical energy that occurs in students with even a shallow awakening.

Objection B: Koan Training Is Too Harsh

"Zen koan training is calculatingly harsh. In sesshin the monitors repeatedly work over the participants with a large stick. This practice reaches a crescendo of beatings and shouts just before the encounter with the roshi, culminating in the "dokusan rush," better called a stampede. In dokusan, the roshi has a smaller stick, which he is not loath to apply to students' backs when they are bowing down before him. Or he will rebuff students with scathing words. How can such harsh practices be reconciled with the Buddhist ideal of compassion?"

Reply

The encouragement stick (*kyōsaku*) is still the favorite whipping boy of Zen's critics, who insist it is "a perversion of Buddhism." Experienced sesshin-goers, however, appreciate it as a welcome goad, especially during those long afternoons of zazen when the energies sink, drowsiness takes over, and the mind teems with unwelcome thoughts. One or two well-directed blows across the flat of the shoulders, at acupuncture meridians, will scatter the most tenacious thoughts and liberate stores of unsuspected energy. For those who are working hard on their practice, the strikings rarely hurt, just as giving the spurs to a fast-running horse will elicit a burst of speed without paining him. Unusually nervous sitters are hardly ever struck, for the monitors know that they will do better zazen without the encouragement stick. Outside of sesshin the stick is used only when a sitter requests it.

But why the heavy use of the kyosaku before dokusan? Long experience has shown that when the stick is used persistently just before the encounter with the roshi, the meeting is more effective. By emptying the mind of the contrails of irrelevant thoughts, it leads to a samadhi-like condition. An individual who reaches this "no-mind" state is verging on awakening and may need no more than a jolt by the roshi, verbal or physical, to precipitate his mind into Self-awareness. The sudden clanging of the dokusan bell affords release from the tension accumulated during the intensive effort at concentration. Simultaneously there is an uncontrollable urge to race to the roshi—to be tested by him or just to present oneself before him.

In the rush to dokusan and in dokusan itself the student expresses a spontaneity that is an essential element of Zen training. Spontaneity is that condition where one is unrestrained by calculation or preconceived notions of how to respond to circumstances. It implies the courage to plunge unreservedly into whatever activity one faces. Most people lead passive lives; they are not the actors but the acted upon. Because they have lost their inborn creativity as free-acting individuals, they can't "let go" unless impelled by strong emotion. In dokusan and in Zen spontaneity is never repressed.

What about the contention that heavy pressures are unreasonably brought to bear on students to achieve a breakthrough in seven days of sesshin? This raises a further question: Is genuine awakening possible in such a short time? Yes, given certain conditions. The seven-day seclusion is the cornerstone of Zen training; in it all the elements of Zen—intensive zazen, the roshi's commentary, and individual instruction—are coordinated into a meaningful whole. With forty or fifty participants striving ardently day and night, sesshin turns into a powerhouse of focused energy. One could call sesshin a process of splitting the atom of the mind to release the stores of untapped energy lying dormant within. Because such energy is indispensable for kensho, the seven-day seclusion is unequaled as a means of achieving a breakthrough.

A disciplined sesshin is one in which the participants do not begin at different times or leave before the end. Freed from outer preoccupations, they can direct all their energies inwardly. During the entire seven days there is no talking or reading. The eyes are kept lowered so that random sights will not disturb concentration. Yasutani Roshi used to say that a taut, coordinated sesshin accomplishes what it would take from two to three years to achieve on one's own. Awakening to one's true nature is the most fundamental realization possible for a human being. Intense inner struggle is necessary to gain control over the mind and then, like a missile, to penetrate the barrier of the five senses and the discursive intellect. To enter this wholly new realm calls for energy, determination, and courage. Yasutani Roshi called it "a battle between the opposing forces of delusion and enlightenment." The Chinese Zen master Po-shan affirmed, "When working on Zen, one never reaches enlightenment merely by waiting for it. One must press forward with all one's mind to get this enlightenment." In the same spirit Zen master Dōgen wrote, "The great way of the buddhas and the patriarchs involves the highest form of exertion. . . . This sustained exertion is not something which men of the world naturally love or desire, yet it is the last refuge of all."

Without force of one kind or another from the outside, not many can accomplish the formidable task of awakening in seven days of intensive meditation; despite a strong aspiration, few can mobilize their dormant energies through sheer willpower. Thus we have the encouragement stick and other forceful aids. Contrary to what many believe, the use of force is not characteristic only of the Zen sect; in Buddhism it goes back to the Buddha himself. In the *Satipatthāna Sutta* he is quoted as saying:

> One should with clenched teeth and with tongue pressing on palate, subdue, crush, and overpower the mind by the mind, just as if a strong man, having taken a very weak man by the head and shoulders, were to subdue him, crush him, and overpower him. Then the harmful thoughts connected with desire, hate, and delusion will disappear.

So force is indispensable—if applied at the right time and in the right way.

In genuine Zen training—and in the use of the encouragement stick—compassion, force, and wisdom are joined. For love without force is weakness, and force without love is brutality. When Zen master Mu-chou slammed the door on the foot of Yün-men, who was trying to force his way into Mu-chou's room for instruction, Yün-men's leg was broken. With a cry of pain Yün-men came to enlightenment. Was Mu-chou compassionate or merely brutal? Later Yün-men castigated Tung-shan for his aimless wandering from teacher to teacher and thereby brought him to awakening. Was that Buddhist compassion or not? A student of mine, referring to the incident of the broken leg, once told me, "Roshi, if you broke both my legs and thereby brought me to awakening, I would be eternally grateful to you. After all, broken legs mend, while a lifetime of practice may not achieve enlightenment."

Pressure, it should be noted, is only one aspect of a Zen sesshin. Like a well-conducted symphony, sesshin has its calm, quiet moods and its crescendos. An able master, like a conductor, directs and blends the diverse movements and sees that none dominates. This variety is also evident in the private encounter. Sometimes the master quietly encourages, at other times he resorts to the "carrot and stick" approach, but without the stick overshadowing the carrot. On still other occasions he shoots fast questions at the student, demanding instant answers. In the zendo, too, there is variety. Sometimes the stick-wielding is heavy, sometimes light, and sometimes conspicuous by its absence. When used, it is *selectively* applied by the monitors, who know the limits of the individual sitters. Especially during the first three days of a sesshin, when the energies are building up, there is virtually no pressure exerted either by the teacher in dokusan or by the monitors in the zendo. It is only during the last four days of a sesshin, when the energies are running high, that the sitters are pressed to exert themselves to the utmost. They discover that they are capable of much more than they ever imagined.

Objection C: Koans Are Artificial and Irrelevant

"The Zen koans are artificial problems imposed from the outside by the teacher. They do not arise from the practitioner's own life situation but from stories of ancient Zen masters. Accordingly, they have little or no relevance to the complexities of contemporary life."

Reply

Undoubtedly the best koan is one that naturally grows out of one's life situation. For example, a Buddhist might be gripped by the following problem: "If all beings without exception are intrinsically perfect, as the Buddha proclaimed, why is there so much imperfection, so much pain and suffering in the world?" Or a believer may question intensely: "If I am fundamentally a buddha, why do I act like anything but one?" Those driven by the need to dispel a fundamental contradiction between their faith in the truth of the Buddha's pronouncement and the evidence of their senses have a natural koan. Similarly, if the question "Where did I come from when I was born and where will I go after I die?" gripped one constantly, it could be another natural koan. I emphasize "could" because not everyone would be motivated to resolve the matter of birth and death. A natural koan is a personal perplexity that gives one no rest.

Strictly speaking, the inquiry "Who am I?" is not a koan, for it lacks a contradictory element, the "bite" that wheedles the intellect into attempting a solution impossible for it. Yet it too can be effective as a spiritual dilemma. At the base of all seeking, whether couched in terms of the "I" or a koan-type paradox, is the desire for self-understanding. If students tell me that the Who? inquiry has been with them since childhood, and that they feel strongly drawn to it, I assign it to them and then give pointers on how to work with it.

In my book *Zen: Dawn in the West* I mention the case of a man who fought in World War II and saw extensive action in the Pacific theater. When he returned to the United States he was utterly beat. In his own words, "I could not work, sleep, or make love." One question obsessed him: "What is reality?" Although his formal education did not go beyond primary school and he had no philosophic or religious inclinations, this question kept biting into him. He would wake up in the middle of the night and the first thing that came into his mind was "What is reality?" Walking along a street he would bump into telephone poles, so absorbed was he in the question. After some six months in this state an explosion took place in him, followed by a tremendous joy. This was his enlightenment. His exhausting war experiences had provided him with a natural koan.

The traditional Zen koans, however foreign they may appear initially, can have just as much impact as a natural koan. The main purpose of an assigned koan is to awaken an aspiration to self-realization that is normally submerged. People are usually propelled into Zen training by profound dissatisfaction with life, a fear of living and a dread of dying. A koan provides a much-needed focus for their spiritual striving and eventually evokes a strong aspiration to awakening. It is emphatically untrue that koans have no relevance to one's daily life. On the contrary, they embody our deepest spiritual concerns; through the struggle to penetrate them they become very real and very intimate. As Heinrich Zimmer points out in *Philosophies of India,* knowledge is the reward of action:

> For it is by doing things that one becomes transformed. Executing a symbolical gesture, actually living through, to the very limit, a particular role, one comes to realize the truth inherent in the role. Suffering its consequences, one fathoms and exhausts its contents.[3]

This passage also expresses the value of koan training. Because koans cannot be theorized about in the abstract, they compel us to feel and act, not merely to talk and think. They liberate us from the snare of language, which fits over experience like a straitjacket; they pry us loose from our tightly held dogmas and prejudices; they empty us of the false notion of self-and-other that distorts our inner vision and our view of the world. How can the realization of such a liberated state be called artificial or irrelevant?

Objection D: Zen Masters Have Too Much Power

"A Zen master is an authoritarian figure with absolute power, nowhere more so than in his teaching room, where all the procedures are weighted in his favor. With an imperious clang of his handbell, he may ring out a student at any time—even in the middle of a bow or a sentence. The bewildered student is given no explanation for this peremptory dismissal. In contrast, the student may not leave when *he* wishes to; he is completely subject to the whims of the master."

Reply

A Zen roshi is not considered by his followers to be an incarnation of a god or some exalted holy figure. If even Shakyamuni Buddha is not looked upon as divine, how much more would that apply to a roshi. One source of his authority is his awakened understanding (and the wisdom and compassion flowing from it). Another source is the sanction to teach he received from his master. Obviously these qualities command a great deal of respect, but they do not compel unquestioning obedience. The Buddha himself affirmed:

> Do not believe anything on the mere authority of teachers or priests. Accept as true and as the guide to your life only that which accords with your own reason and experience, after thorough investigation. Accept only that which contributes to the well-being of yourself and others.

In Zen there are built-in checks which help to restrain a roshi from dictatorial displays of power. The very presence of a twenty-five-hundred-year-old lineage acts as a corrective to individual grandiosity. Moreover, there is a tradition going back to the sixth century in China in which outstanding masters and patriarchs are mocked in a manner that is best described as "praise by slander." Listen to Zen master Wu-men describe Bodhidharma, the First Patriarch of Zen in China and the twenty-eighth in line from Shakyamuni: "that broken-toothed old barbarian who came so importantly from across the seas. He had only one disciple and even he was a cripple." The Buddha receives similar treatment: "Old Shakya put on a clumsy play and was no better than a child." There is wisdom in this attitude of disrespectful respect and respectful disrespect. Its purpose is to bring these great figures down to our level and to prevent us from deifying them. After all, Buddha-nature is common to the lowborn and the highborn, to saints and sinners; if we are willing to exert ourselves mightily as the ancients did, we too can realize our potential buddhahood. But if we look up at them adoringly, they seem so far above us that their achievement of buddhahood appears beyond our reach.

In Zen it is said that the primary role of the master is to protect students from his influence. A good teacher tries to guide himself accordingly. The roshi's aim is not to control the lives of his students but to make them strong enough to lead their own lives with awareness, equanimity, and compassion. While it is also said in Zen that the roshi stands in place of the Buddha, this really means that he manifests the awakened Buddha-nature common to all. In any case, the authority of a roshi over his students extends for a limited period only. When they have completed their Zen training, approached his level of understanding, and "graduated," his authority over them ceases. What remains is the disciples' deep respect and gratitude toward their teacher.

Ken Wilber, who is familiar with Zen training methods, writes in his book *Eye to Eye*:

> I have been a participant-observer in almost a dozen non-problematic new religious movements, Buddhist, Hindu, Taoist. In none of those groups was I ever subjected to any harsh degree of authoritarian pressure (discipline, yes, pressure, no). In fact, the authoritarian pressure in these groups never even equalled that which I experienced in graduate school in biochemistry. The masters in these groups were looked upon as great teachers, not big daddies, and their authority was always that of a concerned physician, not totem boss.[4]

The contention that the roshi's authority is total in the dokusan encounter, as purportedly shown by the fact that he may ring out a student at any time, is based on a misunderstanding of a vital function of private guidance. As pointed out earlier, to be effective a roshi must size up a student immediately and decide intuitively how best to help him or her. If the student's manner perhaps reflects an inflated pride, nothing will deflate the balloon of self-importance faster than a sudden wordless dismissal.

How well I remember the effect of this "fast-bell" treatment administered to me by Harada Sogaku Roshi early in my training in Japan. During a seven-day sesshin I had been having a series of *makyō* (hallucinations) in which I saw the universe dyed in the colors of Paul Klee, only more vivid, more intense, and, paradoxically, more colorless. I was the universe. Only I am, nothing else is. My excitement was unbounded. "This *must* be awakening," I told myself repeatedly in the zendo. As I sashayed into the Roshi's room, brimming with self-confidence and prepared to receive the Roshi's acclaim, he immediately rang me out. I was stunned. My first thought was, "So he doesn't want to sanction a foreigner's enlightenment!" At the next encounter again I waltzed in, my conceit somewhat diminished but still strong enough to communicate itself to the Roshi. As I was in the act of prostrating before him, he clanged his bell. "Out!" it commanded. Back at my mat in the zendo I was boiling mad. Two dismissals in a row with no explanation. This was too much! One more wordless dismissal and I was quitting, I told myself. At my third appearance that day I actually reached the mat in front of the Roshi, having already made my prostrations. As I sat glaring balefully at him, the Roshi suddenly seized his bell and rang me out again.

Back in the zendo, I began to reconsider my own behavior and whether it had any connection with all these peremptory dismissals. My anger started to evaporate, and some self-reflection and humility began to emerge. "You've got too much ego, that's why you were rung out three times, you conceited idiot," I told myself wretchedly. "At your next meeting you must apologize to the Roshi and not even suggest you are enlightened, for obviously you're not." And I did just that.

To come to understand by oneself what is wrong with oneself is always more valuable than to be told it by someone else, even one's own teacher. All this, and more, such Zen treatment can accomplish. Were a student allowed to leave the dokusan room whenever *he* wanted to, the Roshi would be deprived of this invaluable device. The Roshi must be free to push a person down or raise him up, to encourage one and chastise another. The allegation that the personal encounter invests the Roshi with unlimited authority and deprives the student of his rights could only be made by someone unfamiliar with the aims and functions of private instruction in Zen.

Objection E: Basically, There Is Nothing to Teach

"Zen maintains that in an ultimate sense there is nothing to teach and nothing to learn, nothing to seek and nothing to find. As a Zen verse puts it, 'Without raising a foot we are there already. The tongue has not moved, but the teaching is finished.' If this is so, why is there private instruction? Why severe training? Why Zen itself?"

Reply

It is true that in an ultimate sense there is nothing to teach or learn, nothing to know or do. Yet one is not entitled to say that unless one has actually realized down to one's bones the truth of those statements. For truly to know that there is nothing to know is to know a great deal. Spiritual traditions are full of such glittering truths as: "You cannot enter a place you never left"; "The Absolute is a sphere whose center is everywhere and whose circumference is nowhere"; "Who sees not God everywhere sees him truly nowhere"; or "Refrain from seeking buddhahood, since any search is condemned to fail."

These quotations reflect the awakened awareness of the masters. By simply reading them can we dispel *our* greed, anger, and deluded thinking, thereby transforming our lives? Hardly. This is not to say that reading and study are useless. What others have written about their own deep spiritual experiences can be valuable in showing the way and inspiring one in the spiritual quest—up to a point.

The time comes when we need to abandon the armchair for the sitting mat and undertake training under a genuine master. For the Way, to be a Way, must be walked. Religious doctrines remain mere concepts until translated into actions. It is by acting out the profound teachings that we are transformed. As the Buddha himself affirmed:

> It is indeed a fact that salvation cannot come from the mere sight of me. It demands strenuous efforts in the practice of meditation. . . . A man must take medicine to be cured: the mere sight of the physician is not enough.

It is to this end, then, that Zen masters Po-shan, Dōgen, and the rest urge us to exert ourselves to the utmost. Why else the strenuous exertions of the Buddha and the patriarchs if not to see into their own nature? If there were nothing to do, "then Bodhidharma could just as well have written a note of two or three lines and sent it on to China," comments Zen master Hakuin wryly.[5] Instead Bodhidharma risked his life to make the hazardous journey to China and then spent nine years "facing the wall" in meditation at Shao-lin temple. Hakuin goes on to emphasize that "It is an unparalleled ignorance to believe one can become a buddha without seeing into one's own nature."[6]

But having trained oneself in zazen, having gone to many four- and seven-day sesshins, having heard many commentaries by the master, having had numerous private encounters with him, and at last having caught a glimpse of one's true nature, one can finally assert with confidence: "Without raising a foot we are there already. The tongue has not moved, but the teaching is finished."

4. Zen Koans

by Eido T. Shimano

In the West today the meaning of the word *kōan* remains unclear or even mysterious. Although the literal translation of koan is "public case," a precedent or authoritative document, it does little to elucidate the actual substance and function of koan practice. A koan is simply the time and place where Truth is manifest. From the fundamental point of view, there is no time or place where Truth is not revealed: every place, every day, every event, every thought, every deed, and every person is a koan. In that sense, koans are neither obscure nor enigmatic. However, a koan is more commonly understood as a tool for reaching true insight. In the Rinzai Zen sect "koan study" is the symbiosis of koan and *zazen* (meditation) practice as a means to Self-realization.

The process begins when a student with some experience of zazen is given a koan by a teacher. The first koan is most often Jōshū's *Mu*:

> A monk asked Master Jōshū, "Does a dog have Buddha-nature?" Jōshū replied, "Mu."[1]

Traditionally, when this koan is assigned nothing further will be said to the student about it. The teacher will not explain how this short but incomprehensible dialogue is to be worked on, because he recognizes that intellection is the biggest obstacle to Zen experience—at least in the beginning. Nevertheless, the student is expected to present his understanding of the koan at his next *dokusan* (one-on-one meeting with the teacher), as described by Roshi Kapleau in the preceding chapter. Not knowing what else to do, a student might offer some explanation about an ancient story of a traveling monk who asked a certain question, to which the master answered "Mu." To this the teacher will say nothing. His only response will be the ringing of his handbell, signifying, "Go back and work on it some more."

Within a few hours of this first dokusan, the student must return again with a new presentation. So during the intervening periods of zazen he must go over the koan again and again in order to come up with something. But whatever explanation he offers, the teacher refuses to listen. Each time the student is sent back to the meditation hall with the ringing of the teacher's bell. This procedure may continue for quite some time before the student begins to realize that koan study is not intellectual analysis or personal interpretation, but a process of losing oneself in Mu. With this understanding he may one day present his Mu without peripheral explanations. Then, for the first time, the teacher might open his mouth and say, "That's the way." Since the student is not taught in the customary classroom manner, and since there are no books to advise him on how to solve his koan dilemma, it may take a year or more for him to reach this point of understanding.

On the surface it may seem that a year has been wasted, but during this process the student has sat time and again, and his zazen energy has gradually increased. In this case, the deliberate withholding of overt instruction is the best kind of teaching, because the student is not deprived of the opportunity to gain by his own efforts an experience he will never forget. All those days and months of intense struggle are hardly wasted. This is a typical Asian approach, yet the situation differs here in North America. The Western educational system accustoms people to verbal instructions and orientation sessions. Hence koan study for the American student cannot simply be a duplication of the traditional Japanese way of teaching; in this new context some verbal instruction is appropriate. But whichever the way, Japanese or American, sooner or later the student must sit with Mu and *become* Mu, not just think about it.

One problem with koan study, especially in the West, is that many persist in thinking that a koan is something that can be solved through intellection. People expect the koan to make sense or have some meaning that squares with the rational mind. But habitual intellection is precisely what koan training is set up to undermine. To others, Mu is merely the letters "M" and "u," an unfathomable foreign syllable. However, the point is not to think about Mu or to make anything of it, but to focus so persistently on Mu that the mind eventually becomes inseparable from it. This unwavering absorption is also the state of mind most likely to give rise to *kenshō,* a sudden flash of intuitive insight into the true nature of things.

I often ask students three questions involving the verb "become":

"Can a man become a woman?" The answer is "No."

"Can you become the president of the United States?" The answer is often "There is a slight possibility."

"Can you become angry?" The answer is unequivocally "Yes." It is in the manner of this last answer that one "becomes" Mu. This kind of becoming has nothing to do with philosophical abstraction or theoretical probability. Rather, it most intimately relates to one's own experience.

Before kensho one has a lopsided view of things: one only sees the relative and is ignorant of the fundamental nature of reality. Kensho, to state it another way, is to see the order of the universe right side up. My teacher often said, "If you completely break through Mu, the rest of the koans will be unnecessary. Mu is the one, lifelong, life-after-life koan."

Koan language differs from ordinary or conventional language. It is intended to propel one to clear insight by a route independent of discursive thought. For example: "Walk without feet!"

Rationally, it is difficult to grasp the point of being asked to walk without feet. It is an impossible thing to do. Or one may imagine that the koan contains some sort of esoteric teaching or involves magic. Such responses naturally miss the essential point because the koan aims directly at the intuitive, nonrational mind. Everyone knows that in walking we are not even aware of walking with our feet, only walking. But the master does not ask, "Are you aware of your feet when you are walking?" It is through penetrating such nonrational hurdles that one is led to clearer understanding.

Another example of koan language is the following:

> Ummon said, "Look! The world is vast and wide. Why do you put on your priest's robe at the sound of the bell?"[2]

On the face of it, Master Ummon is asking his monks why they follow the monastic routine when the world offers them so many other options. Whenever we hear "why," we respond by trying to come up with some reason: "Because . . ." However, koan study is not a branch of logic. It is designed to take one beyond logic to where there is no "why" and no "because." To clarify this point, let me give a simple example. A young boy asks his father, "Daddy, why does the sun rise from the east?" The father answers, "Because the earth turns." The boy asks, "Why does the earth turn?" The father thinks that he knows and says, "Because of Newton's second law." The son asks again, "Why does that law hold?" At this point the father would most likely say, "Well, that's the way it is." This is exactly the point: no "why," no "because," only that which Buddhists call Suchness. However, when no further explanation is possible, the fear of failure often prevents admission of a simple truth: "That's just the way it is."

One point of koan training is reduction of delusive pride, the belief that we are capable of knowing all the reasons for everything in existence. The simplest of questions "Why are you here?" is unanswerable in the deepest sense as long as we rely on logic and reason alone. Even modern Western students, so clever in debate, will concede that the intellect is limited in coming to grips with such a question. When this limitation is accepted, emancipation is possible. When it is denied, suffering is perpetuated. The dialogue above between father and son is really nothing more than about "why-ness" and "because-ness," and the questioning will remain on that level no matter how far they take it.

Through training and Self-realization, Buddhists come to accept things as they are, and to accept that which one does not or cannot know. Even though the scientific achievements of the twentieth century are indeed remarkable and owe much to the spirit of inquiry, the why/because approach has not, cannot, and will not solve the basic human question "What is man?" And it is in response to this fundamental issue that zazen practice and koan study can be of some help to humanity.

People often want to know how many koans there are altogether. This question can be answered three ways. If the inquiry is about the traditional koan system, it is generally said that there are one thousand seven hundred, though the actual number of koans studied is far less. The second and perhaps most important way to answer the question is that there is only one koan. Whether it is Mu, or the Original Face Before One's Parents Were Born, or the Sound of One Hand, as long as one thoroughly fathoms a single koan, that is it. The third answer to this question is that there are innumerable koans—standing or sitting, laughing or crying, thinking or doing, in life there is not even one event which is not a koan.

Hakuin's Koan System

The koan system prevalent today was first systematized by the eighteenth-century Japanese Zen master Hakuin and his heir Tōrei from the many recorded sayings, doings, and dialogues of the ancient patriarchs of India and China. There are five general categories followed by three further classifications. Hakuin's first grouping of koans is called *hosshin* in Japanese, literally "Dharma-body." We can render this term more freely as "universal oneness." Through these koans the student comes to realize that all existence, animate and inanimate, visible and invisible, is Buddha-nature itself. Things no longer appear to exist separately and independently, but are seen to be one. Only in concept is the phenomenal realm split into manyness, and because of such conceptualization we persuade ourselves of the existence of multitudes of independent entities, each with its own separate being. Through the hosshin koans the practitioner awakens to the true condition of the universe, which is actually none other than one's self.

The most popular hosshin koan is Jōshū's Mu, introduced above. Another example is the following:

> A monk asked Tairyū, "The physical body rots away: what is the hard and fast body of reality?" Tairyū said, "The mountain flowers bloom like brocade, the valley streams are brimming blue as indigo."[3]

The second category according to masters Hakuin and Tōrei is known as *kikan*, which can be translated as "dynamism" or "spontaneity," qualities that result from having thoroughly integrated the hosshin koans into one's own marrow. Kikan koan practice directs one's attention to the commingling of the two aspects of life, oneness and manyness, thereby nurturing spontaneity and freedom. With zazen and this second level of koan practice, then, one comes to know the fundamental equality underlying distinctions. Although there are high mountains and low, man and woman, young and old, clever and foolish, birth and death, and myriads of diversities in the world around us, one is no longer led astray by these superficial differences, by mere appearances.

The best known kikan koan is Tosotsu's Three Barriers:

Master Tosotsu Etsu set up three barriers for his disciples:

1. You leave no stone unturned to explore profundity, simply to see into your true nature. Now, I want to ask you, just at this moment, where is your true nature?
2. If you realize your true nature, you are free from life and death. Tell me, when your eyesight deserts you at the last moment, how can you be free from life and death?
3. When you set yourself free from life and death, you should know your ultimate destination. So when the four elements separate, where will you go?[4]

This koan clarifies the true nature of life and death, normally considered to be entirely different states.

Kikan is the spirit of Zen in action. Without hesitation one knows how to act appropriately, when to say "yes" and when to say "no." Most of the popular Zen stories depict kikan. One excellent example is found in the *Record of Rinzai*:

> Rinzai (Lin-chi) arrived at Bodhidharma's memorial pagoda. The master of the pagoda said to him: "Venerable sir, will you pay homage first to Buddha or first to Bodhidharma?" "I don't pay homage to either Buddha or Bodhidharma," said Rinzai. "Venerable sir, why are Buddha and Bodhidharma your enemies?" asked the master of the pagoda. Rinzai swung his sleeves and left.[5]

Rinzai's actions express a freedom beyond the bonds of conceptual, social, and religious conventions. The special mark of kikan is this spontaneous expression of spiritual insight.

The third category is called *gonsen,* meaning the investigation of words, or the practice of verbal expression. Phrases such as "It's difficult to explain" or "It's impossible to describe" illustrate the limitations of verbal communication. Even such a common expression as "with much gratitude" is difficult to communicate precisely, not to mention what Zen calls the Great Matter. The primary function of this type of koan training is to learn to avoid entanglements in words and to express the inexpressible in a fresh and impactful way.

Gonsen also hints at subtle meanings. For example, the

responses of such Zen patriarchs as Jōshū or Ummon, who were sparing with words, cannot be taken simply at face value. A monk asked Ummon, "What is Buddha?" Ummon replied, "Toilet paper." Unless one's insight is deep one is likely to be misled by such words and miss the true spirit of the expression.

There are many well-known gonsen koans. Here is one:

> Jōshū asked a traveling monk, "Have you ever been here before?" The monk replied, "Yes, I have." Jōshū said, "Have a cup of tea." Jōshū asked another visiting monk, "Have you ever been here before?" The monk said, "No." Jōshū said, "Have a cup of tea." An attendant monk asked Jōshū, "Why do you say 'Have a cup of tea' to one who had visited before and the same thing to one who has come to see you for the first time?" Jōshū called the attendant's name. The attendant replied, "Yes, sir." Jōshū said, "Have a cup of tea."

Another important aspect of training in gonsen koans is learning how to discern whether an expression or response is genuine or not. When someone thanks you, there are several ways to respond: "You're welcome," "It's my pleasure," "Not at all," "Don't mention it." Functionally, these idiomatic expressions may be considered the same. Yet when one is wide-awake in everything one does and says, then each phrase is a crucial expression, clearly revealing one's state of mind. In genuine Zen dialogue a single word has the power to change another's life.

A haiku poem, only seventeen syllables long, can be gonsen—if it is not merely descriptive. Reality or this Great Matter poetically expressed in seventeen syllables is far more than just poetry. Take for example Bashō's haiku:

> Along this way goes no one
> this autumn evening

It may seem as if Bashō merely intended to suggest something of the poignancy of a lonely country road, one autumn evening. Yet he is at the same time evoking the aloneness of the Way—here the Way of haiku; which in a Zen student's case is the Way of

Buddha-Dharma; for an artist, the Way of art; for a scholar, the Way of study. Each Way being complete unto itself, there is no one to depend on, no one to ask for direction, no one to lead or to teach. Indeed, along this Way goes no one. But whether autumn evening, spring day, summer morning, winter night—it makes no real difference. Only "evening" softens the mere literalness of reality: beautiful things tend to have greater impact when intuited on a more subtle level. I believe that gonsen koans gave rise to the Japanese haiku.

There are a few koans which are especially hard to penetrate. These Master Hakuin categorized as *nantō,* the literal meaning of which is "difficult to pass through." The difficulty of nanto is not only a matter of seeing into the koan, but also of integrating the insight one has attained into one's everyday activities. One must absorb these koans as one's marrow and blood, so to speak. Zen practice is a continuous process of reducing egocentricity and developing compassion. The difficulty and never-ending nature of these tasks can be seen in Hakuin's statement: "I experienced great enlightenment eighteen times; as for small ones, I am unable to remember."

A well-known nanto koan is:

> Goso said, "To give an example, it is like a buffalo passing through a window. Its head, horns, and four legs have all passed through. Why is it that its tail cannot?"[6]

Here one must thoroughly realize that the buffalo's head or tail are not the obstacles. In fact, there are no obstacles, and there never were any—from the very beginning the buffalo's head and tail have already passed through, and *are* passing, always passing through, moment by moment. Another nanto koan selected by Hakuin is:

> An enlightened elderly woman once provided a monk with food and lodging for twenty years. Always a young girl served the monk his meals. One day the woman instructed the girl to embrace the monk and ask him, "What are you going to do now?" The girl did

as she was told and the monk responded, "The withered tree leans against the cold precipice; three months of winter without a breath of warmth." The girl reported this to the elderly woman, who said, "I have wasted twenty years of food and lodging." She kicked the monk out and burned down his hut.

Advanced Stages of Koan Training

The next category in Hakuin's system is known as *kōjō* or "crowning" koans. Kojo koans are used to cultivate imperturbability, the mind which remains unshakeable in the midst of everyday turmoil. Deeply developed Zen practitioners are not aroused to anger no matter what the source of irritation or provocation. Although masters may still scold their students (often with considerable ferocity), such actions originate from compassion, not anger. The "angry" behavior of a Zen master passes almost instantly, an event that can be bewildering for a student who has just been scolded.

An imperturbable mind radiates a silent but powerful influence. Joy and a desire to help others will spontaneously arise from it. At this stage one repeatedly and wholeheartedly embraces the four great vows of a bodhisattva:

> However innumerable all beings are
> I vow to save them all;
> However inexhaustible delusions are
> I vow to extinguish them all;
> However immeasurable Dharma Teachings are
> I vow to master them all;
> However endless the Buddha's Way is
> I vow to follow it.

The following is an important kojo koan:

> One day Master Tokusan went down toward the dining room holding his bowls. Seppō met him and asked, "Where are you off to with your bowls? The bell hasn't rung and the drum hasn't sounded." Tokusan turned and went back to his room. Seppō mentioned this to Gantō, who remarked, "Tokusan may be renowned, but he doesn't know the last word." Tokusan heard about this remark and sent his attendant to fetch Gantō. Tokusan asked, "You do not approve of me?" In reply Gantō whispered his meaning.
>
> Tokusan said nothing at the time, but when he ascended the rostrum the following day—how different was his demeanor! Gantō, going toward the front of the hall, clapped his hands and laughed loudly, saying, "Congratulations! Our old man has got hold of the last word! From now on, nobody in this whole country can outdo him!"[7]

Traditionally, a consideration of Master Tōzan's Five Ranks comes next in the koan training sequence. As this material cannot be adequately presented here, I refer the reader to the excellent treatment by Isshū Miura Roshi and Ruth Fuller Sasaki in *The Zen Koan* (New York: Harcourt Brace Jovanovich, 1965), pages 62–72.

Next taken up in advanced Zen training are the Ten Cardinal Precepts as koan practice. These Buddhist precepts can be seen from two perspectives. For example, the first precept, "Do not kill," gives the impression that it just concerns right behavior or morality. While such teaching is needed, those who continue Zen practice and further clarify their insight into emptiness know that, actually, there is no one to do the killing and no one to be killed. From the ultimate standpoint, "Do not kill" also warns us not to fall into the dualistic view of killing versus not killing. However, it would be a misinterpretation to use this view of the precepts as a pretext for immoral transgression or excess.

In contrast to the conventional Western habit of viewing things from the standpoint of good and bad, the Buddhist sees the world—with all its good and evil—just as it is. Fundamentally, the world is neither good nor bad. Without genuine insight, so-called moral perfection is uninformed and hollow. True insight not only leads to the realization that there is no killer and no one to be killed, it also results in the realization that one simply *cannot* kill. Whereas "do not" is an injunction, which may not necessarily lead to enlightened behavior, the "cannot" realization naturally evolves into the deeply rooted stance of "I won't kill."

Yet the line separating "do not" (injunction) and "cannot" (realization) seems to dissolve when we see that we are always killing something. We may decide not to kill animals for food, but what about vegetables? And so on with everything else we destroy and discard. If we obeyed the injunction "do not kill" literally, we could not eat, we would starve to death, thus ending up by taking life anyway. How can we overcome this dilemma? When the need arises to take life or destroy, whether it be animal, vegetable, or inanimate object, one should just dwell on Mu with all one's heart. Thus each moment we are taking life from some form of existence can be an occasion to be deeply aware of our oneness with the universe in Mu.

Maintaining this attitude is the key point of the Five, Ten, Two Hundred Fifty or Five Hundred Precepts. These precepts are not meant to bind or enslave us. Applied *with* Mu insight, they can be a means to emancipation. The Ten Precepts as koan study are no longer just moral injunctions, but constitute a further step on the road toward the complete realization of oneness in our everyday actions. Such realization does not negate the validity of relative values; it simply does not allow relative values to obscure our original freedom, our Buddha-nature.

When the koans on the Ten Precepts are well integrated, the master gives the student what is known as the "Last Barrier." The specific koan used depends on the master, but the purpose is always the same: to eliminate the subtle pride that came with the idea "I have attained something." Unless one can forget one's "attainment," having passed through the koan system of Hakuin and Tōrei is nothing more than a kind of college credit. So this

Last Barrier has the important function of erasing all traces of ego. Most masters do not easily acknowledge that the final koan has been passed, often withholding approval for several years. These days we want to know and do everything as quickly as possible. Zen's approach is different: it teaches us how to be patient, how to know things intuitively, and how to acknowledge that there are things we do not know. Students may object, "Life is so short. Why spend so many years in training, humbled by our ignorance, before we can even begin to guide others?" This relative viewpoint sees life only as a single span of time. With genuine insight into the fundamental nature of Self, one knows that life never ends. It simply changes.

A New Koan System for Westerners?

Having lived in the United States these past twenty-five years, and having guided the koan practice of many American Zen students, I often feel that mere translations of koans from the Hakuin system are inadequate. The Japanese koan system cannot simply be transplanted as is to new soil, or even grafted somehow onto Western stock. The problems arise partially from cultural differences—culture deeply conditions systems of thought and religion. Though American Zen students are sincerely interested in Buddhism, their basic cultural/religious frame of reference has been the Judeo-Christian tradition. Yet koan practice originated in China, where Buddhism, Taoism, and Confucianism prevailed. Even such a famous koan as "What is the meaning of Bodhidharma's coming from the West?" which can be translated easily enough, assumes a background most Westerners lack. If the same question was rephrased as "What is the quintessence of Buddha-Dharma?" or even more idiomatically as "What is This?" the spirit of the koan might be more comprehensible.

My teacher Nakagawa Sōen Roshi and I once planned to select about one hundred koans suitable for Western Zen practitioners, culled from Hakuin's koan system and more familiar Western sources. Material from the writings of Aristotle, Shakespeare, Dostoevsky, Nietzsche, Chekhov, Hesse, Camus, Beckett, Henry James, Schopenhauer, Goethe, and many others might be suitable. We also intended to comment on such koans for the modern age, to compile a new collection for today's students, so that they could appreciate the real taste of koan study. However, Sōen Roshi passed away before this aim could be realized.

It has been my conviction that the three most worthwhile contributions that the East can make to the West are Buddhist thought, zazen practice, and koan study. Buddhist thought is becoming better known, and zazen practice is spreading. Yet only in isolated cases are koans being properly studied. Unless changes are made, the situation is unlikely to improve here in America (or in Japan, for that matter). As an experiment I have chosen a number of koans and potential koans from classic Asian and Western texts. The selection that follows is entirely my own and is predicated on my current understanding of both cultures. I believe that the transmission of Zen Buddhism to the West will be incomplete until its teaching is made more accessible through a new, Western koan system.

Potential Koans from Western Sources

Little flower—but if I could understand what you are, root and all, and all in all, I should know what God and man is.

—ALFRED LORD TENNYSON

I know that without me God cannot live for an instant: if I perish he must needs give up the ghost.

—JOHANNES SCHEFFLER

The eye with which I see God is the very eye with which God sees me.

—MEISTER ECKHART

Thy will be done, on earth as it is in heaven.

—THE LORD'S PRAYER

When God created the heavens, the earth, and creatures, he did no work; he had nothing to do; he made no effort.

—MEISTER ECKHART

Everywhere (in the Psalms) is the exhortation to praise the Lord, and God demands praise from men. *How* are we to praise the Lord?

—C. S. LEWIS

Christ said, "Come unto me, all ye that labor and are heavy laden, and I will give you rest."

—NEW TESTAMENT

Paired Koans from Western and Zen Sources

He that findeth his life shall lose it, and he that loseth his life for my sake shall find it.

—NEW TESTAMENT

O monks, if you die once on the cushion, you shall never die.

—HAKUIN

* * *

A fool sees not the same tree that a wise man sees.

—WILLIAM BLAKE

Followers of the Way, as to Buddha-Dharma no effort is necessary. You have only to be ordinary with nothing to do—defecating, urinating, putting on clothes, eating food, and lying down when tired.

Fools laugh at me, but
The wise man understands.[8]

—RINZAI (LIN-CHI)

* * *

If the doors of perception were cleansed everything would appear as it is, infinite.

—WILLIAM BLAKE

Gantō said, "If you want to know the last word, I'll tell you, simply—This! This!"[9]

—*BLUE CLIFF RECORD,* CASE 51

* * *

Blessed are the poor in spirit, for theirs is the kingdom of heaven. Blessed are the meek, for they shall inherit the earth.

—NEW TESTAMENT

If a man seeks Buddha, he'll lose Buddha; if he seeks the Way, he'll lose the Way; if he seeks the patriarchs, he'll lose the patriarchs.

—RINZAI (LIN-CHI)

* * *

Blessed be he who will snatch up a Babylonian baby and beat its brains out against the pavement.

—PSALMS

Whatever you encounter, slay it at once: on meeting a buddha slay the buddha; on meeting a patriarch slay the patriarch; on meeting an arhat slay the arhat; on meeting your parents slay your parents; on meeting your kinsman slay your kinsman; and you attain emancipation.

—RINZAI (LIN-CHI)

* * *

Great things are done when men and mountains
meet;
This is not done by jostling in the street.

—WILLIAM BLAKE

A monk asked Master Ummon, "Where do all the buddhas and patriarchs come from?" Ummon replied, "Eastern Mountain walks on the water."

—UMMON (YÜN-MEN)

* * *

Then Pilate said to Jesus, "Do you not hear how many things they witness against you?" And Jesus gave him no answer, not even one word.

—NEW TESTAMENT

A monk once asked Master Fuketsu, "Both speaking and silence are concerned with oneness or manyness. How can we be free and nontransgressing?" Fuketsu said:

"How fondly I remember Konan in March!
The partridges are calling, and the flowers are
fragrant."[10]

—*GATELESS BARRIER*, CASE 24

* * *

Therefore I say unto you, Be not anxious for your life, what you shall eat, or what you shall drink; nor yet for your body, what you shall put on. Is not the life more than the food, and the body more than the raiment? . . . Consider the lilies of the field, how they grow; they toil not, neither do they spin; yet I say unto you, that even Solomon in all his glory was not arrayed like one of these.

—NEW TESTAMENT

Seizei said to Sōzan, "I am utterly destitute. Will you give me support?" Sōzan called out, "Seizei!" Seizei responded, "Yes, sir!" Sōzan said, "You have finished three cups of the finest wine in China, and still you say you have not yet moistened your lips!"[11]

—*GATELESS BARRIER*, CASE 10

* * *

And the fire and the rose are one.

—T. S. ELIOT

The master swordsman
Is like the lotus blooming in the fire.

—TŌZAN (TUNG-SHAN)

* * *

My God, my God, why hast thou forsaken me?

—PSALMS

Master Kyōgen said, "It is like a man up a tree who hangs from a branch by his mouth; his hands cannot grasp a bough, his feet cannot touch the tree. Another man comes under the tree and asks him the meaning of Bodhidharma's coming from the West. If he does not answer, he does not meet the questioner's need. If he answers, he will lose his life. At such a time, how should he answer?"[12]

—*GATELESS BARRIER*, CASE 5

* * *

ESTRAGON: Let's go.
VLADIMIR: We can't.
ESTRAGON: Why not?
VLADIMIR: We're waiting for Godot.

—SAMUEL BECKETT

A monk asked Kōyō Seijō, "Daitsū Chishō Buddha sat in zazen for ten *kalpas* (eons) and could not attain buddhahood. He did not become a buddha. How could this be?"[13]

—*GATELESS BARRIER*, CASE 9

5. Master Hakuin's Gateway to Freedom

by Albert Low

Hakuin Ekaku (1686–1769) is widely regarded as one of the greatest masters in the history of Japanese Zen. As the Japanese put it, someone of Hakuin's stature appears only "once every five hundred years." Hakuin almost single-handedly revived Rinzai Zen in Japan by restoring disciplined monasticism and reiterating the centrality of the enlightenment experience. His systemization of koans, outlined by Eido Roshi in the preceding essay, remains influential today. Not only was Hakuin an extraordinary teacher, he was also a gifted calligrapher and a prolific painter.

Hakuin's formal Zen writings fill eight hefty volumes. Yet one of his best-known and most-loved works is a pithy poem called the *Zazen wasan,* or "Chant in Praise of Zazen." This verse is still chanted regularly in Japanese Rinzai monasteries, and now it can be heard in North American Zen centers as well. In this essay I will comment on Hakuin's chant in the Zen manner—striking up against it, so to speak, and letting the sparks fly as they may. One of the purposes of a Zen commentary is to loosen set habits of thought, opinions, and judgments. This letting go is a necessary prelude to the more radical release which is called awakening.

Here is Hakuin's complete "Chant in Praise of Zazen," in a translation favored by Zen practitioners:

From the beginning all beings are Buddha.
Like water and ice,
without water no ice,
outside us no Buddhas.
How near the truth
yet how far we seek,
like one in water crying, "I thirst!"
Like a child of rich birth
wandering poor on this earth,
we endlessly circle the six worlds.
The cause of our sorrow is ego delusion.
From dark path to dark path we've wandered in darkness—
how can we be free from the wheel of samsara?
The gateway to freedom is zazen samadhi—
beyond exaltation, beyond all our praises,
the pure Mahayana.
Observing the precepts, repentance, and giving,
the countless good deeds, and the way of right living
all come from zazen.
Thus one true samadhi extinguishes evils;
it purifies karma, dissolving obstructions.
Then where are the dark paths to lead us astray?
The pure lotus land is not far away.
Hearing this truth, heart humble and grateful,
to praise and embrace it, to practice its wisdom,
brings unending blessings, brings mountains of merit.
And if we turn inward and prove our True-nature—
that True-self is no-self,
our own Self is no-self—
we go beyond ego and past clever words.
Then the gate to the oneness of cause-and-effect
is thrown open.
Not two and not three, straight ahead runs the Way.

Our form now being no-form,
in going and returning we never leave home.
Our thought now being no-thought,
our dancing and songs are the voice of the Dharma.
How vast is the heaven of boundless samadhi!
How bright and transparent the moonlight of wisdom!
What is there outside us,
what is there we lack?
Nirvana is openly shown to our eyes.
This earth where we stand is the pure lotus land,
and this very body the body of Buddha.[1]

The chant starts:

From the beginning all beings are Buddha.

What does "from the beginning" mean in this bold assertion? Does it mean that eons and eons ago we learned all there is to know, that we have somehow carried it through the years, and that we still have it or are it—that we are still Buddha?

Such a view implies that time has a beginning, a notion deeply embedded in our Western culture. Traditionally, Westerners have believed that at some time God made the universe, and that in due course it will come to an end—perhaps with the second coming of Christ. More recently, theoretical physics has developed the idea that it all started with a big bang, and there are others who think it will also end with a big bang. We so naturally assume there is a beginning in time that we are bemused when it is put to us that perhaps there is no beginning or end.

The thirteenth-century Japanese Zen master Dōgen spoke of "being-time." He taught:

> Standing on the peak of a high mountain is time. Diving to the bottom of the ocean is time. The staff and the *hossu* (whisk) are time.[2]

Climbing up the stairs to come into the meditation hall is time. Getting settled on your mat is time. The encouragement stick is time. A modern Zen teacher, Shunryu Suzuki, said:

> There is no such time as "this afternoon" or "one o'clock" or "two o'clock." At one o'clock you will eat your lunch. To eat lunch is itself one o'clock.[3]

The modern philosopher Henri Bergson has an understanding of time similar to Dōgen's. He writes as follows:

> Reality is a flowing. This does not mean that everything moves, changes, becomes. Science and common experience tell us that. It means that movement, change, becoming is everything that there is. There is nothing else; everything is movement, is change. The time that we ordinarily think about is not real time, but a picture of space.[4]

The notions of "beginning" and "end" are a result of conceptualization. In Zen practice we are used to the idea that we have to get beyond thought; it is almost a cliché. We believe that the thoughts we have to transcend are "I like Mary" and "I don't like Jack"—in other words, our temporary judgments. But to get beyond thought we have to get beyond the fundamental idea of *being*, with its correlates of existence, time, and space. As long as we are caught up in the notion of time as a box then we have got such problems as "Where was I before I was born?" Or to put it more abstractly, "Where was I before I was?" Likewise, "Where will I be after I am dead?" or "Where will I be after I am?" And we can only stand paralyzed in the face of these questions. "What is your face before your parents' birth?" is how the Zen koan puts it. How are we going to answer this as long as we are locked in this prison of time?

"From the beginning all beings are Buddha" is a clarion call to wake up. Where is this beginning? When is this beginning? If we cannot put it into the past, if we cannot put it into the future, are we going to say it is the present? When pop philosophers talk about living *in* the "here and now," they have already missed the mark. Fundamentally, there are no things that move and change and become: everything is time.

Let us dwell a bit longer on Hakuin's trenchant opening line:

From the beginning all beings are Buddha.

Good news and bad news. The good news is that we are Buddha; the bad news is that *all* beings are Buddha. The sickness of being human is the sickness of wanting to be unique. Each of us tries to be the only One. Each of us wants to regulate the universe so that it circles around us and around us alone. The idea that we are the same as all the rest of humanity and all beings is something which is almost impossible for us to accept. A basic way of affirming uniqueness is to gain the attention of others. In this sense, the game of being alive is the game of "look at me." If necessary we will seek attention aggressively—by dominating, forcing, using strength. Or we will try to get it by weakness—through submissiveness, inability, even illness.

Some people come to Zen because they think that spiritual practice will at last prove that they are special. Some come to sit longer, better, straighter than anyone else. In certain religions people undertake frightful austerities and use the power that comes from these practices to build up an image of themselves as the One. As long as we think, however secretly, "Won't it be good when I come to awakening?" "Won't it be easy when I am enlightened?" "What will I tell everybody when I come to awakening?" we build up barriers. It is rather the sacrifice of uniqueness, the constant giving up of oneself that leads to awakening. And this work can only be done secretly, quietly, without a lot of fanfare.

The only true way to know ourselves as the inviolate One is to accept the suffering that comes because we are not unique in the way that we would like to be; that indeed we are ordinary in so many respects. The word "humility" comes from "humus," which means the earth. So we must come down to earth. From the beginning *all* beings are Buddha. There is nothing exalted about this truth, nothing exalted in being Buddha. When Dōgen returned to Japan after his awakening in China, he was asked, "What did you bring back from China?" He answered, "My nose is vertical, my eyes are horizontal." Everything is just as it is. Someone has said about awakening, "I walk on my own feet, I see with my own eyes."

Like water and ice,
without water no ice,
outside us no Buddhas.

This water/ice image is similar to the analogy of the clay jug: the jug gives the form, and the clay gives the substance. Here we can say that Buddha is the substance. All our perceptions and conceptions, our consciousness itself, all the things that we see, taste, touch, or feel—these are the forms this substance takes.

The word Buddha comes from a root word that means knowing or awareness. Mountains and trees, houses and factories, cars and animals are all forms of the "clay" of knowing. Everything that we are aware of is awareness itself. Sometimes we say that awareness is like a mirror, and that everything is reflected in it. The room that we see is reflected in the mirror of awareness. Or we could say that awareness is the "substance" of the room. Our belief that we see solid, immutable things comes from our fundamental conceptual framework, especially notions of space and time. But, as Bergson says, everything is flowing. The chair is flowing, the floor is flowing. Or, as Dōgen says, everything is time. Or, as is being said now, everything is Buddha, everything is knowing, awareness. Each of these formulations has a slightly different emphasis, but they are nevertheless saying basically the same thing.

If we look upon awakening as something "out there," something absolute, something that will make us distinctive, then it is too great for us, too difficult for us; only spiritual geniuses can attain it. But once we see that it is knowing, that it is in our very eye, even closer than our eye, then it is no longer something special. Once we recognize that all beings are Buddha, then awakening is no longer something that only the great can achieve.

In cutting the root of the search for uniqueness lies our possibility of freedom. But this search for uniqueness has been with us for a long time; it may even be a driving force of evolution. More than just one hack at the root is needed to destroy it. We should not be alarmed if we look around and see people who have chopped a bit still exhibiting the very things that we ourselves suffer from. The struggle is continuous and continuously painful. But, at the same time, once we have seen into this matter we are no longer locked in the cul-de-sac of ignorance. There is some light. Perhaps it is only very dim at first, but it is light. Buddha is knowing. This is what is so wonderful.

How near the truth
yet how far we seek,

How near the truth indeed! Each one of us, from morning till night, is a continuous flow of knowing, an unending symphony of knowing, a rising and falling of knowing. We are never out of knowing; it is always present. It is a great mystery, and yet there is no mystery to it. The peace that comes from seeing this is not a peace without conflict, but a peace that sees that conflict too is knowing. Birds fly in the air, fish swim in the water, human beings live in knowing. There is an old Hindu song which says, "My Lord is in my eye, that is why I see him everywhere." It could not be any closer. When we breathe in, we breathe in knowing; when we breathe out, we breathe out knowing. That is all there is to it.

Hakuin says, "How near the truth yet how far we seek." Look for yourself. Never mind about all those people who have got this or that. Find out for yourself. When you sit in zazen and breathe out, what is it? When you breathe in, what is it? Never mind what others have to say. *What is it?*

Like one in water crying, "I thirst!"

William James said that the first step in religious life is the cry for help. "I thirst, help me!" Until we realize that we are lost we can never find ourselves. Until we realize that we are sick we cannot seek a remedy. Until we realize that we are asleep we can never wake up. And yet it is in the middle of pure water that we cry, "I thirst!" It is in the midst of pure knowing that we call out, "I don't know who or what I am. Please help me." Knowing itself reveals to us that we are lost, that we are asleep, that we can cry out.

Here, once again, are the opening lines of Master Hakuin's chant:

> *From the beginning all beings are Buddha.*
> *Like water and ice,*
> *without water no ice,*
> *outside us no Buddhas.*
> *How near the truth*
> *yet how far we seek,*
> *like one in water crying, "I thirst!"*

The next line is:

> *Like a child of rich birth*
> *wandering poor on this earth,*

This image is a reference to a well-known parable in the *Lotus Sutra.* The son of a rich man strays from home and wanders in poverty for many years, forgetful of his origins. Eventually he happens to stray near his home again. The father sees the boy but realizes that if he went out and simply said, "You are my son," the boy would be suspicious and afraid. So instead the father arranges for the boy to be employed as a servant of the house. Gradually the son is promoted until the father is sure he is ready to be told the truth.

The parable depicts a person who is heir to infinite riches but constantly in a state of poverty. We might ask ourselves, "What is this great wealth, rightfully ours, that we are constantly overlooking?" Some would respond that it is esoteric wisdom, or a tremendous reservoir of love, or a superconscious state. A Zen koan that goes well with this parable (cited in the preceding essay) can be paraphrased as follows:

> A monk called Seizei goes to a master and declares, "I am poor and destitute, please give me something to sustain me." And the master calls out, "Seizei!" The monk answers, "Yes, master?" The master says, "There, you have nourished yourself and yet you say you are poor and without sustenance."

Each one of us is Seizei, "poor and without sustenance." We may have all the riches in the world, we may be a Rockefeller or a Rothschild, we may own the Apple computer company or be president of the United States, but still we would feel we lacked something. Even if we were given exactly what we think we are missing, it would not be enough. Imagine for a moment that every one of your wishes was granted to you; then what would you wish for? If you had it all, would you be rich?

What does the master mean when he says, "Seizei!"? Supposing you genuinely realize your poverty of spirit, and you go to a teacher and say, "I lack that which is most profound." And he calls you by name: "John!" "Joan!" . . . "Yes," you reply. And he says, "There, you have all the riches you will ever need." What are these riches? There is a step from poverty to fullness that involves neither change nor movement. Until we can take that step we will continue to wander poor on this earth.

We endlessly circle the six worlds.

In the traditional cosmology of Buddhism, the six worlds are those of gods, fighting titans, human beings, hungry ghosts, animals, and hell. Some say these are objective, geographic realms, places to which we can go. Others say they are subjective states that come about through psychological experience. But it may be that they are neither places nor psychological states; perhaps they belong to a kind of intermediate zone which is neither subjective nor objective. In any case, here Hakuin means that as long as our inherent birthright remains unrealized, no realm of existence grants immunity from ignorance or suffering.

The cause of our sorrow is ego delusion.

This matter of ego is old hat now, is it not? People tell us they have lots of problems, and then they add, "Of course, it's because I have got a big ego, I know that." Or sometimes we hear, "He is a nice guy, but he has got a hell of a big ego." What is this big ego? How can an ego be bigger in one person than in another? And how can people so easily and without any sense of remorse view themselves as having a big ego and even proclaim it? The word "ego" is one of those Latin words that seems to have dropped on us from a great height and stunned us. Ego was once just an ordinary word that meant "I." To say "I have a big I" or "He has a weak I" does not make much sense.

What is this word "I"? We take it so for granted, allowing it to slip off the tongue without hesitation and with great frequency. We become especially aware of it after a *sesshin,* or meditation retreat. For several days we have remained silent, and now it comes crowding into our conversation. To experience its strength, it is a good exercise to spend a few hours or a day using the word "I" as sparingly as possible, or even not at all. One feels as if one is giving up some addiction. "I" is so important that people will kill others, or even themselves, in its defense.

"I" is one of the most mysterious words and one of the most expensive. The Indian teacher Ramana Maharshi used to refer all comers to the question "Who am I?" This question also plays a significant role in the Sufi tradition and in Zen.

Krishna says in the *Bhagavad Gita*:

> I am the beginning, the middle, and the end in creation. I am the knowledge of things spiritual. I am the logic of those who debate. In the alphabet I am A. I am time without end. I am the sustainer. My face is everywhere. I am death that snatches all. I also am the source of all that shall be born. . . . In this world nothing animate or inanimate exists without me.[5]

In the Gnostic Gospels we find Christ saying:

> It is I who am the light which is above them all. It is I who am the all. From me did all come forth and to me did the all extend. Split a piece of wood and I am there; lift up a stone and you will find me there.[6]

How then can Hakuin say that the cause of our sorrow is ego delusion? What is the delusory aspect in all of this? The cause of our sorrow is the delusion of "I," and yet it is I who am the light of the world. This is the mystery—this is why "Who am I?" is such an important question. If we can penetrate through "I" to I, we have penetrated through to everything. Here we are not talking about something semantic or psychological. Nor are we talking about something remote or philosophical for great minds to study. We have it right here, so close to us. I. What is I? What is it? Hakuin is simply saying, "Look, there is a problem. You are taking something for granted and so you think you are poor, but you are rich." The ego delusion is the delusion of poverty, the delusion that I is something very important *rather than all that there is.* Why settle just for the good and by doing that completely lose the best? Why settle for a million dollars and forego your human heritage?

> *From dark path to dark path we've wandered in darkness—*
> *how can we be free from the wheel of samsara?*

This couplet, which marks the end of the chant's first section, brings us right down into the valley of death. With it we enter the slough of despond. Those who have read the Psalms will recall that nearly every psalm is saying, "From dark path to dark path I have wandered in darkness; how can I be free from this darkness?" For example, the heart-rending Twenty-second Psalm repeats the cry taken up by Christ on the cross:

> My God, my God, why hast thou forsaken me?
> Why art thou so far from helping me, from the words of
> my groaning?
> O my God, I cry by day, but thou dost not answer;
> and by night, but find no rest.[7]

This lament expresses the dark gloom that seems to be our human lot. And so we ask: How can we find a way out of this darkness? How can we be free from the wheel of *samsāra,* the endless round of conditioned existence?

Hakuin responds in two ways, as does Buddhism generally. One is the *dhyāna* response, and the other is the *prajñā* response.

Dhyana and prajna are key Sanskrit terms; their meaning will emerge as we go on. In the distinction between them lies the essence of Zen teaching. First Hakuin takes up the dhyana aspect and says:

> *The gateway to freedom is zazen samadhi—*
> *beyond exaltation, beyond all our praises,*
> *the pure Mahayana.*

Throughout Zen's long history, spanning many centuries and many cultures, all the masters have concurred that zazen, seated meditation, is the most direct and most wondrous path to liberation. Early Japanese masters called zazen "the Dharma gate of great ease and joy," and Hakuin reiterates that it is the precious "gateway to freedom" for all human beings.

The Japanese phrase *makaen no zenjō,* here translated as "zazen samadhi," has been rendered more literally by Trevor Leggett as "the Zen meditation of the Mahayana," and by D. T. Suzuki as "meditation in the Mahayana practice." *Zenjō* is an East Asian equivalent of dhyana. Sometimes dhyana means *samādhi,* total absorption to the point of self-forgetfulness. Yet sometimes dhyana simply means zazen, or as Suzuki says, "meditation in the Mahayana practice." Whatever ambiguities there may be in the various translations, Hakuin is saying here that the *gateway* to freedom is dhyana—the zazen practice which ultimately leads to samadhi. His praise of zazen continues in the following passage:

> *Observing the precepts, repentance, and giving,*
> *the countless good deeds, and the way of right living*
> *all come from zazen.*

Zen, by its very name and nature, puts zazen above all these other kinds of practice. For Hakuin, all good deeds, all efforts to save people, all the precepts, and all forms of proper living come out of zazen. Of course he is not saying that all of these things are *replaced* by zazen.

Here is one of the areas where Zen runs into a great deal of hot water, especially in the West. I had a discussion not long ago with a person who had been to our Zen center several times. Although intellectually gifted and well-known in his field, he said that he was troubled by a fundamental thirst and hoped to find some kind of relief in Zen. Then he stopped coming. He told me that he felt Zen people are not sufficiently engaged in society, that zazen is very good but that somehow it ducks the main issue. The world is in a terrible state, he said, and there are all kinds of situations calling out to be remedied; to just sit and work on oneself in this way seems very selfish.

Many people make this point, and we should not dismiss it too quickly. Are we retreating from the world's problems or our own through the practice of Zen? Are we seeking meaning only within a closed system? Have we got something that has its own rules, its own rewards, its own status hierarchy? Does "I am practicing Zen" mean "I am now living in a walled city which is safe from the marauding bandits of suffering, hunger, disease, and human cruelty"?

I asked this man what he planned to do, and he said that he was going to read widely and join discussion groups to identify the most critical problems. "Yes, and when you have finished discussing, what are you going to do?" I asked. He replied, "I don't know yet; that is the whole idea of reading and discussing." I suggested that he might want to go to a hospital to work as a volunteer for a few hours a week, or that he go to some lonely person's home, to give that person a couple of hours of company a week. I added that perhaps it would be best to start with one person and a few hours before one went on to save the world. He laughed and said, "I see what you mean. I am avoiding something, aren't I?" The point, of course, is that we can be avoiding something either way. Saying one wants to help others can be just that: saying without any doing, a sentimental way to avoid effort.

When we closely examine the good we try to do, we often find that we are simply looking for some way in which we can be comfortable with the world. As if it were a matter of insurance premiums, we pay with a certain amount of good action and expect to insure ourselves against the vicissitudes of the world. Thus some people, when things get tough, will say, "I don't understand. Why am I getting all these troubles? I have been a good person, lived a good life."

We must nevertheless be very careful here. Zen practitioners sit morning and evening, go to a few sesshins a year, and after that they may feel they have done their thing. After all, doesn't Hakuin say that zazen is most important? But do not miss Hakuin's true meaning: we must keep the precepts, we must do the countless good deeds and make sure we live rightly, yet the only way we can do these things authentically is with a firm foundation of zazen.

Thus one true samadhi extinguishes evils;
it purifies karma, dissolving obstructions.

What does Hakuin mean when he states that one true samadhi purifies karma? Several religions, Hinduism for example, assert that the attainment of samadhi itself purifies karma. Indeed, the teachers whom the Buddha met when he first left home held to this belief, and yet he rejected their teaching. The original text of the chant literally claims that just "one single sitting" purifies karma. Whether we use "one true samadhi" or "one single sitting," on the face of it either assertion seems improbable.

There is a saying that once we are on the Buddha's path, once we are totally committed to seeking the truth, then everything is taken care of. This does not mean that we are not going to suffer any more, but rather that our suffering becomes slanted in an entirely different way. What before was quite brutal or incomprehensible now becomes a way, a door, a call. "A single sitting" refers to the miraculous power that can come about as a consequence of commitment to a spiritual path—not just the Buddha's path but any genuine way that leads to transcendence of the limited self.

The Buddhist sutras tell the story of Devadatta, a cousin and disciple of the Buddha who was so envious of the Buddha that he tried to kill him. Devadatta's karma condemned him to the deepest hell. While he was lying there in anguish, Buddha sent two disciples with the following prediction: "You will remain in the deepest hell for one *kalpa* (eon). After suffering for that period of time you will then be able to become a buddha." The next line of the account is crucial: "Devadatta's joy was profound." He responded:

> If this is so, if I should be able to become a buddha after one kalpa, although the time be one of unbearable suffering, I will place myself in the midst of this hell of incessant suffering, throughout the time resting on one side (without even turning over) and with so completely relaxed a disposition will endure the whole of the suffering.[8]

However hellish one's situation may be, if one can open oneself to the truth that intrinsically one is already whole and complete, lacking nothing, then one's life will be transformed from that moment on. Once we realize that our suffering itself is in some way a door to this truth, then our life is no longer the same. In a fundamental sense, we have purified our karma, dissolved our obstructions. This is not to say that now we do not have to live out our karma, or that we do not have to work with those obstructions; but it means that our relationship to them is totally different. The Zen poet Ryōkan asks, "If you point your cart north when you want to go south, how will you arrive?" Hakuin is telling us that with one sitting we can point the cart south.

> *Then where are the dark paths to lead us astray?*
> *The pure lotus land is not far away.*
> *Hearing this truth, heart humble and grateful,*
> *to praise and embrace it, to practice its wisdom,*
> *brings unending blessings, brings mountains of merit.*

This truth that we are whole and complete is something that cannot be repeated too often. Let us open ourselves to it humbly and gratefully, getting the sense of it, feeling the glory of it, taking it into ourselves as our own. *We are whole and complete just as we are; we do not need to change a thing.*

Yet Hakuin does not stop here. The chant goes on, this time to the second response, which we called the response of prajna, or awakening.

> *And if we turn inward and prove our True-nature—*

We must *prove* our true nature, know it beyond any question or doubt. This knowing is as intimate as knowing whether the water you drink is hot or cold. It is of no use for someone else to tell us that we have this true nature or to tell us that we have seen into it. That would be like someone coming up to you and saying, "Great, you have got a million dollars in the bank! Congratulations!" and then walking off. And you say, "Good God, he didn't tell me the name of the bank or the account number."

The English expression "turn inward" is perhaps unfortunate because some people then ask, "Where is in?" (A more literal translation is "turn and face oneself.") If I hear a bird singing, have I turned inward or outward? If I acknowledge my feelings of anxiety, have I turned inward or outward? Is there an inward and an outward? We must not be taken in by these terms; they are just pointing.

> *that True-self is no-self,*
> *our own Self is no-self—*
> *we go beyond ego and past clever words.*

These words hold a very deep truth. They refer to a self which *is* self. But this self is best described as "no-self" so that we do not cling to any notion of some thing that exists, believing that to be the self.

We can only say "Our True-self is no-self, our own Self is no-self" with a great deal of humility, with respect for all those who have worked on language in the past. We should never let it slip off the tongue lightly. Unfortunately, Zen has been around long enough for us to get used to such expressions as no-mind or no-self. Arthur Koestler even hacked at Zen Buddhism because he felt that it used a kind of Orwellian newspeak, avoiding serious issues by saying that good is evil, self is no-self, and so on. Our language is a beautiful instrument that has taken thousands of years to evolve. Anyone who has struggled to define a word, or to come up with the word that fits a situation exactly, or coin a word to express something new can begin to appreciate the agony of all the people who have labored to temper the sword of language. So we must be very careful not to take this sword and just pound it against a stone.

The concluding section of Hakuin's chant is a lyrical and joyous evocation of deep enlightenment. The gate opens; the Way runs straight ahead; nirvana is revealed in wisdom's transparent light; and this earth becomes paradise itself. The path to all these marvels, the wondrous gateway to freedom, is none other than zazen. If we have now gotten "past clever words," perhaps we can spare Hakuin the entanglements of further commentary. Just listen to the singing and dancing of his powerful Dharma voice:

> Then the gate to the oneness of cause-and-effect
> is thrown open.
> Not two and not three, straight ahead runs the Way.
> Our form now being no-form,
> in going and returning we never leave home.
> Our thought now being no-thought,
> our dancing and songs are the voice of the Dharma.
> How vast is the heaven of boundless samadhi!
> How bright and transparent the moonlight of wisdom!
> What is there outside us,
> what is there we lack?
> Nirvana is openly shown to our eyes.
> This earth where we stand is the pure lotus land,
> and this very body the body of Buddha.

6. Zen Poetry

by Burton Watson

According to an early work of the Chinese Ch'an or Zen sect, Hung-jen, the Fifth Patriarch of Chinese Zen, gave instructions that each of his disciples should write a verse so that he could judge the student's level of understanding. The majority of the disciples lacked confidence to do so, and it remained for the head monk, Shen-hsiu, to compose a verse and inscribe it on a wall where it would come to the master's attention. His verse read:

The body is the tree of wisdom,
the mind a bright mirror in its stand.
At all times take care to keep it polished,
never let the dust and grime collect!

Later Hui-neng, who had been working in the threshing room and had not yet received instruction from the master, composed two verses of his own. Since Hui-neng did not know how to write, he had someone inscribe the verses on the wall for him. The first one read:

Wisdom never had a tree,
the bright mirror lacks a stand.
There never was anything to begin with—
where could the dust and grime collect?

The master, realizing the outstanding quality of Hui-neng's understanding, summoned him in secret and handed over to him the robe that symbolized the transmission of the teachings. Thus Hui-neng in time came to be recognized as the Sixth Patriarch of Chinese Zen.

The historicity of this account, found in the *Platform Sutra of the Sixth Patriarch* (*Liu-tsu t'an ching*), is examined by Dr. McRae in the next chapter. What concerns us here is the fact that, at least by the time the text was composed in the eighth or early ninth century, it was the practice in the Zen school to use verses in Chinese to express doctrinal ideas and levels of enlightenment.

The two verses quoted above are identified in the text as *chi,* a Chinese transcription of the Sanskrit word *gāthā,* which in Buddhist writings indicates a verse written to praise the Buddha or to summarize the gist of a prose passage in the sutras. In Chinese these poems consist of four lines of five characters each, with rhymes at the end of the second and fourth lines.[1]

Although Zen Buddhism generally agrees in its basic tenets with the other schools of the Mahayana tradition, two characteristics are particularly marked in its teachings. First is the tendency to brush aside elaborate doctrinal theories and to urge the student to concentrate directly upon the basic enlightenment experience. Second is the demand that the student view enlightenment and its implications in terms of his own immediate situation. Thus when Zen employs poetry to give expression to its ideas or outlook it prefers brief, highly compact poetical expressions that are suggestive rather than expository in nature. Zen poetry usually eschews specifically religious or philosophical terminology in favor of everyday language, seeking to express insight in terms of the imagery and verse forms current in the secular culture of the period. The poems quoted above, occurring very early in the Chinese Zen tradition, are more overtly philosophical than is characteristic of Zen poetry as a whole, but in form they are indistinguishable from the secular poetry of the time. In the examples from later periods that will be quoted hereafter, one will see even this mildly doctrinal note largely disappearing, at least from the surface level of the poems. This deliberate avoidance of technical religious terminology is a reflection of the Zen belief that one has not fully grasped the significance of enlightenment until one can manifest it in the language of daily life.

Varieties of Zen Poetry

The poems from the *Platform Sutra* cited above were written by students to express their level of understanding, and poems of this type continued to be composed in later periods of Zen history. Similar in nature are the poems written by a Zen master for a particular student, a kind of certification that the student had attained a satisfactory level of enlightenment. Such poems were customarily presented when the master granted *inka,* the official seal of approval that allowed the disciple to become a Zen master in his own right. These two types of poems, since they deal specifically with the content and degree of enlightenment, tend to be more technical in language than other types of Zen poetry.

Another somewhat specialized category of poems are those which Zen masters in China, Korea, and Japan have composed as appreciations or comments on *kōan.* Well-known examples are the verses written by the Chinese monk Hsüeh-tou (980–1052) to go with the koans in the *Blue Cliff Record* (*Pi-yen-lu*), or the similar verses appended by Hui-k'ai (1183–1260) to the koans in his *Gateless Barrier* (*Wu-men-kuan*). Verses of this kind employ a variety of line lengths. They tend to be so laced with irony and cryptic in utterance—the writer naturally does not want to give away the answer to the koan—that they require elaborate explanation.

Ceremonial occasions provided the stimulus for another type of Zen poetry. For example, the following poem was meant to be recited at dawn of the eighth day of the twelfth lunar month, the date when Gautama or Shakyamuni Buddha was believed to have attained final enlightenment as he gazed at the morning star. The ceremony marking this event continues to be held in major Zen monasteries in Japan, usually at the end of a week-long period of intensive training, and poems of this type are written each year for recitation. This example is by the Japanese monk Gidō Shūshin (1325–1388), a leading figure in the "Literature of the Five Mountains" (*gozan bungaku*), works written in Chinese by medieval Japanese Zen monks. The poem is a quatrain with seven characters in each line.

Before dawn, the Morning Star, night after night;
over the hills, twelfth-month snow, year after year:
how laughable—to suppose Gautama did something special!
Quick, let's notch the gunwale so we can find the sword!

The last line alludes to a Chinese story of a man who dropped his sword overboard while riding in a boat; he put a notch in the gunwale at the place where the sword fell into the water so he would know where to look for it later. Gidō implies that it is equally fatuous to concentrate upon the enlightenment gained by a particular historical figure, Gautama, at a particular time in the past, instead of seeking to realize the Buddha-nature inherent within oneself.[2]

Another type of poem much used in Zen circles is the verse inscription written to accompany a picture, usually one depicting some figure or anecdote in Zen lore. Sometimes the inscription is written by the artist himself; at other times it is added by another hand. The following example, a Chinese verse in five-character lines, is by the Japanese monk Ikkyū (1394–1481). It was written to accompany a painting by Soga Dasoku (d. 1483) of the Chinese Zen master Lin-chi, who was famous for employing shouts and beatings to help his students toward enlightenment.

Shout for shout, shout for shout for shout—
that instant tells if it's life or death!
Wicked devil, his ogre eyeballs
bright, bright as any sun or moon![3]

The following poem was also written to accompany a painting, this one a *chinsō* or formal portrait of a Zen master such as was often presented to the master's disciples. The portrait, painted at the request of a woman lay believer, was of the Japanese monk Jakushitsu Genkō (1290–1367), an outstanding poet of the Gozan literature, and the poem that accompanied it is by Jakushitsu himself. Such portraits customarily depicted the master wearing full priestly robes and looking very solemn.

> Who took these splendid robes of purple and gold,
> wrapped them round the old fool's lump of red flesh?
> When bystanders see him, I'm afraid they'll laugh—
> better send him back to stay in his old green mountain![4]

In addition to such specialized contexts, poems were written on many other occasions in the life of the Zen monastery, just as they were used on numerous social occasions by members of the educated class in general. Chinese scholar-officials customarily exchanged poems of parting when one of their number set off on a journey, and the same practice prevailed among the Zen monks of China and Japan. The following is such a poem of farewell by the Japanese monk Nampo Jōmyō (1235–1308), better known by his title Daiō Kokushi. It is entitled "Sending My Attendant Shin off to Hōshū" and is in seven-character quatrain form. The attendant, Sōshin Sokuan (d. 1351), was going to a temple called Manjuji in Bungo (Hōshū). In the poem Daiō Kokushi offers his disciple some advice on how to proceed in the search for enlightenment.

> I'm old, no strength to keep calling three times.
> I leave it to autumn winds to help get things moving.
> When you've left here, look as you stand by Bungo Castle stream:
> Yellow leaves tumbling in the air—for whose sake do they fly?[5]

The first line alludes to the seventeenth koan in the *Gateless Barrier,* which reads: "The National Teacher [Nan-yang Hui-chung] three times called to his attendant, and three times the attendant answered. The National Teacher said, 'I was about to conclude that I had let you down. But on the contrary, all along it was you who let me down.' " Interpretations of this koan differ. Some commentators believe that the National Teacher's words are to be taken at face value and that he was genuinely disappointed at the lack of vitality in his attendant's response. Others see his words as an expression of approval—in Zen ostensible condemnation often indicates praise. Unfortunately there is no way to tell how Daiō Kokushi himself interpreted the koan. In the second line, the phrase translated "help get things moving" is literally "help stir up workings." "Workings" are the workings of enlightenment or the enlightened mind. The autumn winds help the process of instruction by posing the question in the last line, which should lead the student to ponder the relationship between himself and the rest of the phenomenal world.

Like Daiō Kokushi's poem, the following is intended to offer instruction to a disciple and nudge him along toward an understanding of "this thing," enlightenment. It is by Jakushitsu Genkō, the first of "Two Poems to Show to a Monk."

> This thing—I show it to you clear as can be!
> No need to plot any special feats or exploits.
> Breezes mild, the sun warm, yellow warblers caroling;
> spring at its height already in the blossoming treetops.[6]

Zen monks frequently traveled about from temple to temple, and like so many travelers in East Asian cultures they employed poems to capture the scenes of their journey. The following poem by a Chinese Zen monk known as Master Feng of Pei-shan (n.d.) describes a visit to Kuo-ch'ing-ssu, a famous temple in the foothills of the T'ien-t'ai range in Chekiang Province. The temple is associated in legend with Han-shan or the Master of Cold Mountain, an eccentric recluse-poet who lived nearby and often came to the temple to beg leftovers. He is said to have inscribed his poems "on trees and rocks," hence the allusion in the last line. The poem is from the *Collection of Styles of the Zen Monks* (*Chiang-hu feng-yüeh chi*), a Chinese Zen anthology compiled in the mid-thirteenth century.

> Outside the temple, already I know how fine the mountain must be;
> clear cool shade detains me—I sit by the circling balustrade.
> On newly opened leaves I see insect inscriptions,
> wonder if they're from Han-shan's brush, the ink not yet dried.[7]

The next poem, from the same anthology, is by the Chinese Zen master Hsü-t'ang Chih-yü (1185–1269) and is entitled "Listening to Snow." It belongs to a very large category of Zen poems that are addressed to no one in particular but depict the quiet, meditative life of the writer and his state of inner enlightenment. Such poems are frequently characterized by images suggestive of coldness, clearness, and silence, or of idleness and drowsing.

> Cold night, no wind, bamboo making noises,
> noises far apart, now bunched together, filtering the pine-flanked lattice.
> Listening with ears is less fine than listening with the mind.
> Beside the lamp I lay aside the half scroll of sutra.[8]

In a similar vein is the following poem by Jakushitsu Genkō. Here the themes of quietude and seclusion are joined by those of old age and death. This quatrain is the second of "Two Poems Written on the Wall at Mount Konzō."

> Wind buffets the waterfall, sending me cold sounds.
> From peaks in front a moon rises, the bamboo window brightens.

Old now, I feel it more than ever—so good to be here in the mountains:
die at the foot of the cliff and even your bones are clean![9]

There was one other occasion which prompted Zen believers (and followers of other Buddhist schools as well) to compose poems, namely, the approach of death. To be sure, death did not always grant the leisure required for such compositions, and some persons deliberately declined to compose a deathbed poem. When the famous Japanese monk Takuan (1573–1645) was pressed by his disciples for one, he responded by writing the single word "dream." Yamaoka Tesshū (1836–1888), a swordsman and a lay teacher of Zen, wrote the following poem on the verge of death. Whereas the poems quoted up to now have all been in Chinese and written by monks, Tesshū's verse is in Japanese, in haiku form.

Stomach swollen,
and in the midst of this pain,
the crows at dawn

It is said that Tesshū's disciples expressed considerable disappointment that their teacher in his final hours was not able to rise above the level of his physical discomfort, until it was pointed out to them that Zen does not teach one how to rise above the world, but how to live in it.

The Relation between Zen and Poetry

In view of the important role that poetry plays in the literary traditions of both India and China, it is not surprising that Buddhists in those countries should employ poetic forms to voice their religious beliefs. Most of the major sutras contain sections in verse, and verse was often used for later works of a doctrinal or devotional nature. But the writing of poetry posed problems for the Buddhist believer, because Buddhist teachings often express a radical distrust of language in general. For example, in the *Lankāvatāra,* a sutra that was highly influential in the early development of Chinese Zen, the Buddha declares, "Words are not known in all the Buddha-lands," and "What one teaches, transgresses; for the truth is beyond words."[10] And in the *Vimalakīrti Sutra,* when the sage Vimalakīrti is queried about the nature of nonduality, the concept that lies at the core of Mahayana Buddhism, his answer takes the form of a thunderous silence. As is well known, this distrust of verbal expression was especially pronounced in the Zen sect, which described its teachings as "not depending upon the written word, a separate transmission outside the sutras."

When the Fifth Patriarch asked his disciples to write verses expressing their understanding, he may have been trying to get them to forget the doctrinal language of the sutras and to formulate their ideas in contemporary language through the medium of secular verse. Yet it is easy to see how such a request might lead to an unhealthy striving for literary skill and eloquence. As though to warn against such a danger, we are specifically told that the future patriarch Hui-neng "did not know how to write" and hence was not likely to become dangerously infatuated with poetic composition. But later Zen monks did at times take a great interest in the writing of poetry, and many evidently felt twinges of guilt as a result. In Chinese Zen, and at a later date in Japanese Zen as well, an excessive concern with literary expression brought about, or at least was concurrent with, a marked decline in religious zeal.

This matter greatly troubled the Chinese monk Chiao-jan (730?–799?), a distinguished poet and author of a critical work on poetics. According to his biography, in his late years "he decided to give up the writing of poetry, believing that it was not proper for a practitioner of Zen." Vowing to "speak no more words" but to devote himself entirely to meditation, he ceased his literary endeavors and ordered his disciples to take away his writing brushes and ink stone.[11]

One of the most eminent literary figures to comment on this dilemma was the T'ang poet Po Chü-i (772–846). Though Po had a very active career as a government official, in private life he was an enthusiastic student of the Southern School of Zen. During a period of exile in the Mount Lu area of Kiangsi and after his retirement from public service, he spent much time practicing Zen meditation and carrying out other religious activities. In a quatrain written around 818 and entitled "Idle Droning," he confesses:

> Since earnestly studying the Buddhist doctrine of
>   emptiness,
> I've learned to still all the common states of mind.
> Only the devil of poetry I have yet to conquer—
> let me come on a bit of scenery and I start my idle
>   droning.[12]

And in a poem written in 840 and sent to the monks of two temples on Mount Lu where he had previously practiced Zen, he reiterates:

> Gradually I've conquered the wine devil, no more getting
>   hopelessly drunk;
> but I still go on making mouth karma, not having ceased
>   writing poems.[13]

Though Po's confessions may strike one as somewhat light-hearted in tone, as do many of his poems on religious matters, he seems to have been seriously concerned about the amount of time and energy he expended on the writing of poetry and the "attachment" that this passion for literary expression represented. Evidence of this attitude is found in the prose statement that he composed in 839 when he deposited a copy of his writings in the library of Hsiang-shan-ssu, a temple in Lo-yang he often visited. There he avers that it has long been his hope that "these worldly literary labors of my present existence, these transgressions of wild words and fancy phrases, may be transformed into causes that will bring praise to the Buddha's doctrine in age after age to come, into forces that will turn the Wheel of the Law."[14]

Po Chü-i's rather airy wish that his secular writings might miraculously be changed into works of religious merit, sincere though it may be, probably did not strike many people as a realistic solution to the problem. In the later years of the Sung dynasty, when Chinese Zen had lost much of its religious vitality and monks increasingly concerned themselves with poetry, painting, calligraphy, and other arts, a second and much subtler form of escape from the dilemma began to take shape. Reflecting a general tendency of the time to endorse metaphysical or expressive theories in both literature and painting, critics began comparing the enlightenment gained by the Zen student with the poet's ability to grasp the nature of reality intuitively and render it in his work. At first, Zen enlightenment was put forward merely as a metaphor for poetic insight or genius, but as the theory gained in acceptance writers were soon speaking as though the Way of Zen and the Way of Poetry were one, or claiming that the writing of poetry was as much a part of Zen practice as sitting in meditation. The best known early statement of the theory is found in *Ts'ang-lang's Remarks on Poetry* (*Ts'ang-lang shih-hua*) by the late Sung critic Yen Yü (active 1180–1235). A much later and more extreme expression appears in the preface (dated 1483) to the *Kishūdan*, an anthology of Chinese poems in quatrain form compiled by the Japanese monk Ten'in Ryūtaku (1421–1500). This work states that "Outside of poetry there is no Zen, outside of Zen there is no poetry."[15] Because such views seemed so different from earlier Zen attitudes toward literature, they at times evoked fierce reactions among Chinese and Japanese Zen masters, some of whom condemned all poetic activity on the part of monks.

The Japanese gained their knowledge of Buddhism through Chinese translations of the sacred texts and through exegetical works in Chinese; when they came to compile their own commentaries and hagiologies they customarily cast them in the medium of classical Chinese. Thus the Japanese had already begun writing poetry in Chinese on Buddhist themes long before the introduction of the Zen teachings to Japan around the end of the twelfth century. Early Japanese students of Zen in many cases gained their knowledge of the sect either by traveling to China to study in mainland monasteries or by studying under Chinese Zen masters who had come to Japan. Since Zen stresses the importance of personal contact between master and disciple rather than the study of written texts, these early Japanese monks had a strong incentive to learn to speak Chinese, or at least to write the colloquial language with sufficient fluency to be able to carry on "brush talk" with their teachers. Even in later times, when native Japanese Zen masters were plentiful, great emphasis continued to be placed on language facility, and the ability to write acceptable prose and poetry in Chinese came to be looked on as a gauge of the individual's level of religious understanding.

Both the early Chinese masters in Japan and their Japanese successors repeatedly warned against inordinate attention to literary accomplishments. The famous master Musō Soseki (1275–1351) scornfully described monks who devoted their time to such endeavors as mere "shaven-headed laymen" who ranked below the lowest of his disciples. But as religious fervor ebbed and more persons were drawn to the monasteries for other than spiritual reasons, rigorous religious training increasingly gave way to interest in artistic or scholarly pursuits. Indeed, encouraged by critical pronouncements assuring them that Zen and poetry were essentially compatible, monks came to regard such pursuits as one of the prime expressions of Zen life. Skill in the composing of poetry in Chinese became a means of gaining renown within  monastic circles, and even perhaps of attracting the notice of the secular world. By the fifteenth century at least some of the monks in a prominent Kyoto monastery were spending their time during the evening meditation session thinking up clever couplets in Chinese.[16]

While Chinese verse forms, particularly the quatrain, have remained popular till the present, many Japanese Zen writers also turned to native forms of poetic expression. Musō Soseki was a distinguished writer of works in *tanka* ("short song") form, some of which were included in imperially sponsored anthologies. Numerous Zen teachers in more recent times have employed the tanka, haiku, and other forms, particularly when they wished to speak to the general public. An example of such works is the much-recited "Chant in Praise of Zazen" (*Zazen wasan*) by Hakuin (1686–1769), elucidated by Mr. Low in the preceding essay. This text, incidentally, offers its own justification for poetry by declaring that once enlightenment is attained, "our dancing and songs are the voice of the Dharma."

The Literary Value of Zen Poetry

In the preceding pages I have discussed some of the principal types of poetry composed by members of the Zen community, noting the ethical and religious problems that such literary endeavors entailed. In conclusion, I would like to consider what literary values are to be found in this body of Zen poetry—whether one interprets the rather amorphous term "Zen poetry" to mean works written by monks, nuns, and lay believers of the Zen sect, or works that in some way embody the spirit of Zen teachings.

Some such works, for example Hakuin's "Chant in Praise of Zazen," are so specialized in nature that, as Arthur Waley said of the similar Chinese poem "On Trust in the Heart" (*Hsin-hsin-ming*), they are best regarded as versified statements of doctrine rather than actual poems. But many other works clearly demand to be judged as literary endeavors rather than mere expositions of belief, and we must therefore ask to what degree and in what ways they succeed as such.

A poem by the fourteenth-century Japanese monk Tesshū Tokusai begins:

> All the ten thousand *dharmas* spring from a single source:
> what theme shall I take for my song's inspiration?[17]

Since Zen writers believed that all phenomena of the mundane world (dharmas) were part of a single underlying unity, one might suppose that they could choose any theme or object whatsoever for their poems to give expression to that unity. In actual practice, however, they tended to be highly conservative in their choice of theme and imagery, relying on certain stereotypes to evoke the desired response in the reader. The monk's rustic retreat, its simple decor, and its genial surroundings served aptly to symbolize the meditative state of the writer's mind, his emancipation from worldly values and entanglements. The traveler's garb and the road he trod suggested the path of religious striving; the birds and fountains and blossoming trees of a mountain setting betokened companionship with the elements of nature. Powerful emotion, even if recollected in tranquility, was customarily rejected as inappropriate to the enlightened mind, and overt philosophizing (except in expressly doctrinal works) was equally shunned. A personal note was sometimes struck, but usually only in connection with certain symbolically significant activities such as begging for alms, drinking tea, reading, or dozing. Novelty, when it was sought at all, took the form of ingenious variations of the stock themes rather than any broadening of the thematic material itself.

All this made for a body of poetry that is studiedly calm, low-keyed, and lacking in individuality, adroit in its handling of a particular range of imagery but in the end curiously limited. While certain elements of the Zen spirit find literary expression, somehow the freedom that is the essence of enlightenment gets lost.

Or so it seems when one is reading the works of run-of-the-mill Zen writers of China and Japan. Fortunately, certain poets have at times succeeded in transcending these limitations and producing works that are of indisputable literary interest and distinction. In the pages that remain I offer translations of three writers who show us what Zen poetry is like at its best.

The first poet to be quoted is the Chinese recluse Han-shan, mentioned earlier. Though Han-shan was a Buddhist who embraced the basic tenets of the Mahayana tradition, it is not certain just what connection he had with the Zen sect. Nevertheless, his works have been highly prized in Zen circles in both China and Japan; in fact they are regarded as among the finest literary embodiments of Zen enlightenment. Han-shan probably lived during the late eighth and early ninth centuries. Apparently he had a wife and family before retiring to Cold Mountain to live the life of a hermit. All the poems attributed to him, some three hundred in number, are untitled. He does not hesitate to be emotional on occasion, and his poetry is characterized by great thematic variety.

1

My father and mother left me a good living,
I needn't envy the fields of other men.
Clack-clack—my wife works her loom;
jabber jabber goes my son at play.
I clap hands, urging on the swirling petals;
chin in hand, I listen to singing birds.
Who comes to commend me on my way of life?
A woodcutter sometimes passes by.

2

I climb the road to Cold Mountain,
the road to Cold Mountain that never ends.
The valleys are long and strewn with stones,

the streams broad and banked with thick grass.
Moss is slippery, though no rain has fallen;
pines sigh but it isn't the wind.
Who can break from the snares of the world
and sit with me among the white clouds?

3

Last night in a dream I returned to my old home
and saw my wife weaving at her loom.
She held the shuttle poised, as though lost in thought,
as though she had no strength to lift it further.
I called. She turned her head to look
but her eyes were blank—she didn't know me.
So many years we've been parted
the hair at my temples has lost its old color.

4

I wanted to go off to the eastern cliff—
how many years now I've planned the trip?
Yesterday I pulled myself up by the vines,
but wind and fog forced me to stop halfway.
The path was narrow and my clothes kept catching,
the moss so spongy I couldn't move my feet.
So I stopped under this red cinnamon tree—
I guess I'll lay my head on a cloud and sleep.

The Japanese poet Ryōkan (1758–1831) was a great admirer of Han-shan, as the first poem below indicates. A monk of the Sōtō branch of Zen, Ryōkan never headed a temple. He lived in a succession of small retreats in the countryside of northwestern Japan, where he spent his time begging, meditating, reading, and writing poetry. On alms-gathering expeditions he frequently stopped to play with the village children, tossing a *temari* handball or engaging in tugs-of-war with long stalks of grass. Ryōkan wrote in both Chinese and Japanese, employing a variety of forms, and he was highly regarded as a calligrapher. These two poems are in Chinese; both are untitled.

1

Done with a long day's begging,
I head home, close the wicker door,
in the stove burn branches with the leaves still on
them,
quietly reading Cold Mountain poems.
West wind blasts the night rain,
gust on gust drenching the thatch.
Now and then I stick out my legs, lie down—
what's there to think about, what's the worry?

2

Green spring, start of the second month,
colors of things turning fresh and new.
At this time I take my begging bowl,
in high spirits tramp the streets of town.
Little boys suddenly spot me,
delightedly come crowding around,
descend on me at the temple gate,
dragging on my arms, making steps slow.
I set my bowl on top of a white stone,
hang my alms bag on a green tree limb;
here we fight a hundred grasses,
here we hit the *temari* ball—
I'll hit, you do the singing!
Now I'll sing, your turn to hit!
We hit it going, hit it coming,
never knowing how the hours fly.
Passersby turn, look at me and laugh,
"What makes you act like this?"
I duck my head, don't answer them—
I could speak but what's the use?

You want to know what's in my heart?
From the beginning, just this! just this!

The next three poems by Ryōkan are in Japanese. The first is in *chōka* or "long song" form; the others are in *tanka* or "short song" form.

3

On slopes
of Mount Kugami
holed up for winter—
day after day the snow
goes on falling
till trails show no sign
of a soul passing by
and no word comes
from people at home:
so I shut my gate
on the drifting world
and here with this one thread
of clear water from the crags
straight as the string
plucked by the carpenters of Hida
I keep myself alive
through another year,
another today
I go on living

4

Water to draw
brushwood to cut
greens to pick—
all in moments when morning showers let up

5

Dew on it,
the mountain trail will be cold—

before you head home
how about
a last drink of saké?

Taneda Santōka (1882–1940) was a failure at various jobs, an alcoholic, separated from his wife and son. At the age of forty-two he attempted suicide. Pulled from the path of an oncoming train, he was taken in by the head of a local Zen temple, and in time he became a priest of the Sōtō Zen sect. He spent the remainder of his life living in quarters provided by friends or tramping around the country on begging expeditions. His drinking remained a problem to the end; as one writer put it, "saké was his koan," and he never solved it.[18] But the poems and diaries he wrote in his later years, reflecting the extreme poverty, simplicity, and loneliness of his life, have won wide acclaim. His poems are in "free haiku" form, which means they do not observe the traditional 5-7-5 syllable pattern.

1
Buried in weeds
one roof
one man

2
I was given it
it was enough—
laying down my lone chopsticks

3
I go on walking
higan lilies go on blooming

4
Men and women in the bath,
shouting back and forth
over the partition

5
Wish I had a drink!
sunset sky

6
Here in the stillness
of snow falling on snow

7
Now it's burned,
these are all the ashes
left from my diary?

8
Falling away behind me,
mountains I'll never see again

7. The Story of Early Ch'an

by John R. McRae

Much of what we read about Chinese Zen (Ch'an) is full of memorable stories. Bodhidharma upstaging Emperor Wu, Hui-k'o cutting off his own arm, Hui-neng besting Shen-hsiu in a verse competition, Nan-ch'uan killing a cat—all these stories are used to exemplify different aspects of Ch'an. Sometimes the point of the episode is left unstated, as if the effort required to fathom the implicit message will contribute to the reader's spiritual awareness. This tendency to explain Ch'an by means of anecdotes involving aspirants and masters has long been part of the tradition itself. The famous maxim that Ch'an "does not rely on words" refers not to words *per se* but to dead words—words that lack the immediacy of a human story. Indeed, Ch'an lives through its unique collection of stories.

As vehicles of moral and spiritual instruction, these accounts have important didactic uses in the context of the meditation hall. Tools devised and refined by the early Ch'an masters, they are used to bore, cut, plane, and join practitioners. Rather than looking at such stories through the eyes of Zen trainees (real or potential), we can also use them to deepen our understanding of the origins and evolution of the tradition. Here I will focus on one of the most important of the early episodes, to see what it reveals and what it conceals about the historical development of Ch'an.

The Story of the Platform Sutra

The intriguing narrative found at the beginning of the *Platform Sutra of the Sixth Patriarch* (*Liu-tsu t'an ching*), which Professor Watson has summarized in the preceding chapter, is one of the most widely quoted anecdotes in all of Ch'an literature. According to this text, when the Fifth Patriarch Hung-jen (600–674) realized he was near the end of his life, he urged that each of his disciples compose a "mind verse" demonstrating the level of his enlightenment. If one of these verses manifested a true understanding of Buddhism, its author would receive the Fifth Patriarch's robe and would be recognized as the Sixth Patriarch. All but one of Hung-jen's students ignored the master's instructions. The others assumed that the most senior among them, Shen-hsiu (606?–706), would write an outstanding verse and be declared the Sixth Patriarch. After all, did he not function as their instructor in the Dharma? For his own part, though, Shen-hsiu was hesitant:

> The others won't present mind verses because I am their teacher. If I don't offer a mind verse, how can the Fifth Patriarch estimate the degree of understanding within my mind? If I offer my mind to the Fifth Patriarch with the sole intention of gaining the Dharma, it is justifiable; however, if I am seeking just the patriarchship, then it cannot be justified. That would be like a common man usurping a saintly position. But if I don't offer my mind then I cannot learn the Dharma.[1]

Eventually Shen-hsiu did compose a verse, but he was so unsure of its worth and his own intentions in seeking the patriarchship that he inscribed it anonymously on one of the monastery's corridor walls. Working late at night so that no one would see him, Shen-hsiu wrote:

> The body is the tree of wisdom,
> the mind a bright mirror in its stand.
> At all times take care to keep it polished,
> never let the dust and grime collect!

When the Fifth Patriarch saw the verse he praised it highly and ordered his students to recite it. His private response to Shen-hsiu, however, was not so positive. Hung-jen pointed out that the verse did not display true understanding and suggested that the senior monk write another verse in order to gain the Dharma. Shen-hsiu was unable to do so.

In the meantime, an uneducated layman from southern China named Hui-neng (638–713) was at work threshing rice, completely unaware of the Fifth Patriarch's instructions about the future succession. When one day an acolyte passed by the threshing room reciting Shen-hsiu's verse, Hui-neng realized immediately that its author did not understand the "cardinal meaning" of Buddhism. The boy explained the entire matter to Hui-neng, who asked to be led to the corridor wall on which Shen-hsiu's verse was inscribed. There he dictated his own poetic statement:

> Wisdom never had a tree,
> the bright mirror lacks a stand.
> Fundamentally there is not a single thing—
> where could the dust and grime collect?[2]

The Fifth Patriarch's reaction to this verse was quite different from his response to Shen-hsiu's verse. In public Hung-jen denigrated Hui-neng's verse, but late that night he called the layman into the lecture hall and expounded the *Diamond Sutra* to him. Even though Hui-neng was an illiterate outsider from the far

South, he possessed an innate capacity for understanding and was thus immediately awakened to the profound meaning of the scripture. Hung-jen transmitted the sudden teaching and the robe (the symbol of patriarchal succession) to Hui-neng, who left the monastery in secrecy that very night. The illiterate yet enlightened Hui-neng had been made the Sixth Patriarch instead of the heir apparent, Shen-hsiu.

Readers who already know the *Platform Sutra* story no doubt also know that it is interpreted in Ch'an as the archetypal episode in the conflict between the teachings of sudden and gradual enlightenment. This interpretation was first stated in the writings of Tsung-mi (780–841), a noted Ch'an and Hua-yen theoretician. According to Tsung-mi, Shen-hsiu taught:

> Although sentient beings are in fundamental possession of Buddha-nature, it is obscured and rendered invisible because of their beginningless ignorance. . . . One must depend on the oral instructions of one's teacher, reject the realms of perception, and contemplate the mind, putting an end to false thoughts. When these thoughts are exhausted one experiences enlightenment, there being nothing one does not know. It is like a mirror darkened by dust—one must strive to polish it. When the dust is gone the brightness (of the mirror) appears, there being nothing it does not illuminate.

Hui-neng's understanding is regarded as superior to Shen-hsiu's because it can be achieved by anyone in a sudden and complete transformation. The assertion in Hui-neng's poem that "fundamentally there is not a single thing" is valued as a practical expression of the teaching of *śūnyatā*, the essential emptiness or nonsubstantiality of all things.

In the usual interpretation, the verses also represent another significant conflict, based on the assumption that Shen-hsiu and Hui-neng were the leading figures of the Northern and Southern groups, respectively. This view holds that the verse competition is an allegory for the historical struggle between these two schools and the eventual ascendance of the Southern school. After an initial period of popularity, the Northern school was supposedly overwhelmed and driven into extinction by the Southern school, which was inherently superior because the true transmission had gone to Hui-neng rather than to Shen-hsiu.

Traditionalists may be disappointed to learn that the *Platform Sutra* account is completely inaccurate as history and that the conventional interpretation errs at almost every point. First, the biographies of Shen-hsiu and Hui-neng reveal that the two men were not at Hung-jen's side at the same time, and probably neither of them was with him near the end of his life. Hence an exchange of verses between Shen-hsiu and Hui-neng, or any other form of competition between the two men for the succession to Hung-jen's position, simply never happened.

Second, the two verses cannot be simplistically interpreted as representing opposed gradual and sudden positions, or as having some kind of symbolic accuracy with regard to the teachings of Shen-hsiu and Hui-neng. We now know that Shen-hsiu did *not* advocate a gradualist method of approaching enlightenment, but rather a "perfect" teaching that emphasized constant practice. Although Hui-neng probably did espouse the sudden teaching, it was not exclusively a Southern school doctrine; in fact, it was presented in the context of *Northern* school ideas until the fourth decade of the eighth century.

Third, it is illegitimate to consider the verses separately, since they clearly form a single unit. That is, the verse attributed to Hui-neng is not an independent statement of the idea of suddenness but is heavily dependent on the verse attributed to Shen-hsiu. I believe that the unnamed author of the *Platform Sutra* wrote the verses as a matched pair in order to circumscribe a single doctrinal position. (In fact, the original author drafted two versions of "Hui-neng's" verse, both of which were slightly different from the later version given above.)

Fourth, the *Platform Sutra* was written around the year 780, more than a century after Hung-jen's death, and the story of the verse competition is not known in any earlier source. Hence the image of Hung-jen's community and the contest he supposedly set in motion are not valid for the end of the seventh century but must rather be understood within the context of late eighth-century Ch'an. Finally, there is good evidence that both verses—including the famous line, "Fundamentally there is not a single thing"—were strongly influenced by Northern school sources. Scholars can no longer accept the view of this phrase expressed by D. T. Suzuki when he called it "the first proclamation made by Hui-neng" and "a bomb thrown into the camp of Shen-hsiu and his predecessors."[3]

The Story's Background and Its Protagonists

During the seventh century Ch'an developed at a specific mountain site in south-central China. In 624 a monk named Tao-hsin (580–651), who is remembered as the Fourth Patriarch of Ch'an, took up residence at Huang-mei in what is now Hupeh Province. Tao-hsin's biography indicates that he selected this site because of its natural beauty, but other evidence suggests that he may have been invited there by the man who was to be his major heir. This successor was Hung-jen, the Fifth Patriarch, who presided at Huang-mei from Tao-hsin's death in 651 until his own death in 674. During the half-century that the two men operated this alpine retreat, an ever-increasing number of students came to study meditation under them; eventually it was said that eight or nine out of every ten spiritual aspirants in China had visited the site. The students were of diverse backgrounds, ranging from Pure Land devotees to *Vinaya* (monastic code) specialists, from exegetes to ascetics. While at Huang-mei they devoted themselves exclusively to meditation.

This period of steady growth was continued for another quarter-century (675–700) at Yu-ch'uan-ssu, the nearby monastery of Hung-jen's most important disciple, Shen-hsiu. Hence for fully three-quarters of a century, from Tao-hsin's arrival at Huang-mei in 624 until Shen-hsiu's departure from Yu-ch'uan-ssu in 700, Ch'an existed in the form of relatively isolated alpine monastic communities.

I believe that the Fifth Patriarch Hung-jen was the central figure during this period. We have too little information about Tao-hsin to be able to say much about him, but it would seem that the major increase in the movement's popularity came during Hung-jen's years of supervision. The most common term for Ch'an during the early eighth century was the "East Mountain Teaching," derived from the location of Hung-jen's monastery at Huang-mei. Hung-jen was described by contemporary followers as a quiet, unassuming man, not disposed toward doctrinal exposition or scriptural study but always on the mark in his personal instructions to students. For years he supposedly meditated with the monks by day and slept with the cattle at night.

Hung-jen's disciples attributed to him the teaching of *shou-hsin* or "maintaining (awareness of) the mind," and it is probably valid to accept at least the core of this idea as his. The underlying rationale for this teaching was the idea of Buddha-nature immanent within all sentient beings, described by the metaphor of the sun:

> There is an adamantine Buddha-nature within the bodies of sentient beings. Like the sun, it is essentially bright, perfect, and complete. Although vast and limitless, it is covered by the layered clouds of the five *skandhas* (aggregates). Like a lamp inside a jar, its light cannot shine.

The text compiled in Hung-jen's name by his disciples, the "Treatise on the Essentials of Cultivating the Mind" (*Hsiu-hsin yao lun*), also recommends a distinctive type of meditation practice. Rather than labor to strip away the illusions that obscure the Buddha-nature, the meditator is instructed to nurture his awareness of the Buddha-nature within, visualizing it like the glowing orb of the sun. Through such practice the illusions will eventually fall away of themselves. Thus the image of the Buddha-nature as the sun of enlightenment shining within is used in two ways at once: to urge students on to greater faith and effort, and to restrain them from conceptualizing enlightenment as something external to be "acquired."

The next protagonist we encounter in the *Platform Sutra* story is Shen-hsiu. He is depicted as learned and sincere—but not fully enlightened. What do we know about this man's biography? Although Shen-hsiu was not necessarily Hung-jen's most intimate disciple, he was certainly the most important in purely historical terms. Born into a very prominent family, perhaps with a direct connection to the T'ang ruling house, Shen-hsiu was known for the breadth of his learning:

> He could converse in the southern dialects of Wu and Chin and was thoroughly versed in the exegesis of the mysterious principle of Lao-tzu and Chuang-tzu, the great truths of the *Book of Documents* and the *Book of Changes*, the sutras and *śāstras* (treatises) of the Three Vehicles, and the rules of the Four-part Vinaya.

After traveling to the famous mountain centers of Chinese Buddhism, Shen-hsiu studied under Hung-jen for six years (651–657). Although the evidence is circumstantial, it seems that Shen-hsiu was influential in an extended and highly politicized debate at court in 662. He defended the right of monks to refrain from doing obeisance to their parents or the emperor. Shortly afterward Shen-hsiu was banished from the capital, and he spent the rest of his life at Yu-ch'uan-ssu monastery in Ching-chou. For the Ch'an school Shen-hsiu's banishment may well have been fortuitous, because he gathered a great number of able students around him during this period. His efforts at court on behalf of Buddhism must have increased his prestige among the religion's followers.

In the year 700, Shen-hsiu was invited to the imperial court of Empress Wu. Although this invitation is largely ignored in the traditional lore of Ch'an, it may have been the one historical event that did most to determine the Ch'an school's future course of development. Empress Wu, it should be noted, was a unique figure in Chinese history. Some years before inviting Shen-hsiu to court she had used Buddhism to bolster her reign, identifying herself as a virtuous bodhisattva whose peaceful rule had been prophesied in scripture. She had skillfully combined these politico-religious claims with effective but harsh administration; by 700 she was at the peak of her power and was thus able to offer Shen-hsiu sincere religious devotion without any obvious political overtones. When Shen-hsiu arrived in Lo-yang, Empress Wu welcomed him in an extraordinary manner—she had him carried into the palace on a special palanquin, and then she prostrated herself before him.

During the next five years Shen-hsiu taught the "East Mountain Teaching" of Hung-jen throughout the two capitals of Ch'ang-an and Lo-yang. As one contemporary author described it:

> Students of Buddhism from the two capitals and the faithful from all areas of China come to the Imperial City to hear his teaching. They come from a thousand miles away without any hesitation! The mendicants with their robes and begging bowls crowd into newly built halls like schools of jumping fish; their huts cover the hillside like lines of geese. Gathering like clouds and free as the dew, they go to Shen-hsiu empty-handed and return fulfilled.

After Empress Wu and Shen-hsiu died within a few months of each other in 706, Shen-hsiu's successors continued to receive extensive support from the imperial house. Although the level of patronage declined after Emperor Hsuan-tsung was enthroned in 712, Shen-hsiu's successors remained prominent. Shen-hsiu's most important disciple, P'u-chi (651–739), accompanied Emperor Hsuan-tsung on his journeys back and forth between Lo-yang and Ch'ang-an and taught meditation to a large number of students. The momentum achieved during these early decades of the eighth century enabled P'u-chi's lineage to flourish until the beginning of the tenth century.

Probably during his Yu-ch'uan-ssu period Shen-hsiu wrote a text called the "Treatise on the Contemplation of Mind" (*Kuan-hsin lun*). He explained the contemplation of the mind using the metaphor of a votive lamp that is never extinguished:

> When one's wisdom is bright and distinct, it is likened to a lamp. For this reason, all those who seek emancipation always consider the body as the lamp's stand, the mind as the lamp's dish, and faith as the lamp's wick. The augmentation of moral discipline is taken as the addition of oil. Wisdom, bright and penetrating, is likened to the lamp's flame. If one constantly burns the lamp of true enlightenment, its illumination will destroy all the darkness of ignorance and stupidity.

Rather than simply maintain one's awareness of the Buddha-nature within, one is to assume innate enlightenment and work to have it function perfectly in all moments of consciousness.

What do we know about Hui-neng, the third major protagonist of the *Platform Sutra* anecdote? The answer to this question may be surprising: virtually nothing. Hui-neng's name first appears in the historical record in a list of Hung-jen's disciples. That source describes Hui-neng as a master of regional significance in far-off Ts'ao-ch'i (in modern Kwangtung Province). His name also occurs in a fanciful piece in which various Ch'an luminaries gather around Hung-jen's *stūpa* or memorial pagoda to discuss the "mysterious principle" of Buddhism. Thus Hui-neng was remembered initially as a student of Hung-jen and as a lesser figure within the community of masters that we now refer to as the Northern school.

Hui-neng's name would almost certainly be forgotten today were it not for the efforts of his student Shen-hui (684–758). Shen-hui (who does not appear in the *Platform Sutra* anecdote and should not be confused with Shen-hsiu) trained for a few years under Hui-neng at Ts'ao-ch'i. Then in the last decade of the seventh century he traveled north to take an official ordination at Ch'ang-an. It was probably at this time that he spent three years studying under Shen-hsiu, but he eventually returned to Ts'ao-ch'i to be with Hui-neng during the latter's final years. Hui-neng is said to have acknowledged the increased spiritual maturity that Shen-hui gained during his years of study in the North, and Shen-hui's understanding probably matured further during his years of wandering after Hui-neng's death in 713. Initially Shen-hui seems to have maintained good relations with the students of Shen-hsiu and other prominent successors to the Fifth Patriarch Hung-jen.

During these years of activity in the North, Shen-hui presented the teachings he inherited from Hui-neng in the context of ideas that we now associate with the Northern school. But in public lectures held in 730, 731, and 732, Shen-hui vigorously proclaimed his independence from these ideas and attacked the legitimacy of the Northern school. He argued that the true transmission of Buddhism had not proceeded through the Northern school lineage from Hung-jen to Shen-hsiu to P'u-chi, but was instead held uniquely by the Southern school of Hui-neng. In fact, it was Shen-hui who first coined the term "Northern school" and applied it pejoratively to Shen-hsiu's student P'u-chi. Shen-hui described the Northern school teachings as:

> freezing the mind to enter meditation, fixing the mind to view purity, activating the mind to illuminate the external, and concentrating the mind to realize the internal.

What is the fault in such a formulation? Shen-hui believed that the teaching of sudden enlightenment he had received from Hui-neng was incompatible with the types of mental contemplation practiced by his contemporaries in the North. Criticizing these practices as compartmentalized yogic endeavors, Shen-hui rejected the gradualist notion that one should improve oneself through meditation until one achieved enlightenment.

The doctrine with which Shen-hui is most closely identified, and which he may well have inherited from the historical Hui-neng, is the sudden teaching. Indeed, Shen-hui's sermons were given with a palpable sense of immediacy, and it is apparent that he wanted to lead those in attendance to experience an initial awakening even as they listened to him. An evangelist who specialized in speaking from the ordination platform, Shen-hui regarded this first instant of enlightenment as the most important point in the spiritual quest.

Solving the Riddle of the Platform Sutra

It may seem that with Shen-hui we have discovered the immediate basis for the *Platform Sutra* anecdote. Accordingly, most modern scholars have assumed that the *Platform Sutra*'s story of the exchange of verses between Shen-hsiu and Hui-neng can be taken as allegorically if not historically accurate, expressing doctrines legitimately associated with the Northern and Southern schools and the two men. Further, those doctrines are thought to indicate an enduring paradigm for the divergence of religious teaching within the Ch'an tradition. Unfortunately, the matter is more complex, and its solution is not quite at hand.

The first stereotype that must be rejected is that of the triumph of Shen-hui's mission. The existence of the *Platform Sutra* cannot be taken as a measure of his success, since there are significant differences between Shen-hui's doctrines and the positions taken in this text. In 796 Shen-hui was supposedly recognized by the imperial court as the Seventh Patriarch, but he is not accorded this rank within the Ch'an tradition itself. In fact, Shen-hui's own lineage died out long before the lineage of the Northern school masters he attacked.

Shen-hui's greatest impact was not directly related to his doctrinal claims regarding suddenness and gradualism or his version of the transmission from Hung-jen to Hui-neng. Rather, he was most influential in the area of Ch'an rhetoric. Shen-hui was a master storyteller; he inspired his congregations with exciting new anecdotes about Bodhidharma, Hui-k'o, and other early patriarchs. The popularity of his stories helped Ch'an to focus attention on the words and deeds of individual masters and to adopt a more colloquial style of expression. In addition, Shen-hui's censure of the Northern school for its alleged gradualism, tantamount to an accusation of dualistic conceptualization, made later masters hesitant to express their ideas in any fashion that might be vulnerable to similar criticism. In other words, Shen-hui's anti-Northern school campaign pressured the Ch'an school as a whole into adopting a rule of rhetorical purity that avoided formulations with any appearance of dualism.

The crisis in Ch'an fomented by Shen-hui was resolved by the Ox-head school and the *Platform Sutra*. The Ox-head school gets its peculiar name from its origins at Mount Ox-head in southeastern China; all its known members were from the South, and they operated chiefly in a small area of modern Kiangsu. Rather than a close-knit community of masters and students training together, the Ox-head school appears more to have been an abstract religious ideal to which different individuals subscribed. One of its doctrinal missions was to defuse the factionalist rivalry created by Shen-hui's campaign. Thus we read that the Ox-head school considered itself a "separate teaching outside of the two schools." Its members believed that the division into Northern and Southern schools was "an error of speech," and that "North and South reviled each other like fighting tigers, shoulder-to-shoulder, and the Way became hidden." The *Platform Sutra* emerged from this milieu in part as a response to Shen-hui's campaign. The text may paint an uncomplimentary picture of Shen-hsiu, but its only mention of Shen-hui is as an unenlightened and smart-alecky youth; Shen-hui's role as a propagandist for Hui-neng is ignored. Undoubtedly, one purpose of the *Platform Sutra* account was to provide a rationale for Hui-neng's identity as Sixth Patriarch without reference to Shen-hui.

A reexamination of the *Platform Sutra* "mind verses" reveals considerable Ox-head and Northern school influence. The phrase "not a single thing" appears frequently in Northern school literature. There are close parallels between the favored Northern school metaphor of the lamp (as in the Shen-hsiu passage cited above) and the metaphor of the mirror in the two famous verses. And the pairing of the two poems suggests a characteristic pattern of Ox-head school doctrine: the statement of a doctrinal proposition followed by an immediate denial that usually indicates a more profound level of understanding.

One of the lessons we can learn from this inquiry is that in Ch'an lore things are not as they appear; indeed, the reality is often contrary to appearances. Though Shen-hsiu was pivotal in the history of Ch'an, his biography was simply too well-known for him to be transformed into a legendary hero. The elegant courtiers of the early eighth century were impressed by his interpretations of Buddhism, his transcendent demeanor, and his ascetic longevity, but by the time the *Platform Sutra* was written three-quarters of a century later, the glories of Shen-hsiu's life had faded. The attraction of Hui-neng was that he was the antithesis of everything that upper-class society cherished: he was from the far South; he had no education or social standing; and he was not even a monk. The figure of Hui-neng represents a prototypic religious antihero, a legendary image that could develop only because Hui-neng's actual biography was almost entirely unknown.

Twentieth-century scholars have used all available resources, including the newly discovered Ch'an texts from Tun-huang in northwest China, to fill out the story of Ch'an transmission from Bodhidharma onward and to provide more complete images of the individual masters whose names are included in the lineage. I have called this the "string of pearls" approach to Ch'an because the underlying goal of such endeavors is to create a sequence of vivid snapshots of the patriarchs, each with his own biography and set of teachings, much like a beautiful necklace of identical pearls. Alas, from the standpoint of history we find that the pearls are illusory and the necklace only a convenient fiction. There is virtually nothing that is known about Ch'an during the seventh century that does not come down to us filtered through the perspective of the eighth century or later periods.

Although some may despair upon discovering that the Hui-neng of Ch'an lore is a legendary figure, the importance and validity of the *Platform Sutra* account is not compromised by its fictive nature. On the contrary, the literary and religious significance of this text and its engaging central character may be enhanced by the absence of historical veracity. Like Bodhidharma and Hui-k'o before him, and Ma-tsu and Lin-chi after him, Hui-neng is in part a creation of the collective Chinese religious imagination. As a spiritual ideal generated from the aspirations of early Ch'an practitioners and embraced by subsequent generations, the legendary image of Hui-neng has a deeper and more intimate relationship with Ch'an and Chinese culture than an essentially random historical account could ever have. Historically accurate or not, the story and figure of Hui-neng, and the traditional version of the conflict between the Northern and Southern schools, continue to be vital aspects of Ch'an/Zen teaching.

8. The Development of Japanese Zen

by Philip Yampolsky

Although advocates of Zen, both in Japan and in the West, often present it as something that stands apart from historical reality, the Zen institution has its own complex history, and the religion has significantly affected the cultures of China, Japan, and other nations. However transcendental the experience of enlightenment, it is embodied in particular individuals; however timeless the truths of Zen teaching, they are expressed in specific historical contexts.

Ch'an (Zen) Buddhism began to emerge as a separate school in early eighth-century China, as Dr. McRae's essay has shown. Although Japanese Buddhist monks visited China in the eighth and ninth centuries and brought back to Japan some of the teachings of this new form of Buddhism, it did not immediately catch hold. Most schools of Buddhism emphasize meditation, and perhaps this recent variant did not appear sufficiently novel to the Japanese. By the Southern Sung dynasty (1127–1279), however, Zen had become the dominant school in China; in fact, virtually all Buddhism was Zen. Thus when Japanese priests visited Sung China it was natural that they should most frequently encounter Zen monks, who were in charge of all the important temples.

The standard interpretation of Zen history in Japan attributes the introduction of Rinzai Zen to Myōan Eisai (Yōsai, 1141–1215) and the introduction of Sōtō Zen to Dōgen Kigen (1200–1253). Later developments are then traced from these two pioneers. The true story is more complex, for there were many other figures who also played significant roles in the development of Japanese Zen.[1]

Eisai entered Buddhism in 1154 at the Tendai center on Mount Hiei, where he studied the exoteric and esoteric doctrines taught by that school. Going to China for the first time in 1168, he visited the holy places of Tendai. On his return Eisai advocated the reform of his own school in terms of a strict maintenance of the Buddhist precepts. In 1187 he paid a second visit to China, remaining there for four years until he had obtained acknowledgment of his enlightenment from his Zen teacher Hsü-an Huai-ch'ang (Kian Eshō, n.d.). Back in Japan, Eisai established temples in Kyushu, Kyoto, and Kamakura, where he introduced some Zen teachings—often in the face of opposition by the entrenched Tendai establishment. Yet Eisai remained in all respects a Tendai priest, determined to reaffirm the precepts as an essential part of Tendai teaching. Of the many books Eisai wrote, only one was devoted to Zen.

While Eisai was in China on his second trip, a priest who purported to be a Zen master, Dainichi Nōnin (?–1196?), began to teach in the area around Kyoto. Because traditional sources have largely ignored this figure, and in light of materials that have surfaced recently, his case merits our attention here. Nōnin's group came to be known as the Nihon Daruma (or "Japanese Bodhidharma") sect. Like Eisai, Nōnin had originally studied Tendai Buddhism on Mount Hiei, but he became dissatisfied with it and proclaimed himself to be a self-enlightened Zen teacher. Very little is known of Nōnin's life. The only extant biographical sketch is from the Tokugawa period (1603–1868). This passage, with its condensed drama and sectarian bent, exemplifies the documents that historians of Zen try to elucidate:

The priest Nōnin's other monastic name was Dainichi. He was the uncle of Kagekiyo, the leader of the Taira family. While young he attended lectures and studied the sutras and *śāstras* (treatises). By nature he was attracted to Zen. Polishing his talents, he meditated deeply and eventually attained enlightenment. He erected Sambōji temple in Mita in Settsu, where he spread the Zen teaching widely. Monks and laymen of the Kinki area flocked to him. He was attacked, however, because he had not studied under a master.

Therefore, in 1189 he sent his disciples Renchū and Shōben, bearing a letter and gifts, to Sung China. The disciples offered these items to the Ch'an master Cho-an (Fo-chao) Te-kuang (Settan Busshō Tokkō, 1121–1203) of A-yu-wang-shan, requesting that he acknowledge their master's understanding. Te-kuang gladly attested to Nōnin's awakening and sent him a Dharma robe, a name, and a picture of Bodhidharma with a verse-in-praise inscribed. Renchū and Shōben had an artist paint a portrait of Te-kuang and asked the master to write a verse. Te-kuang wrote: "This monk, a true man without face, has upset the heavens and turned back the axis of the earth. Master [Nō]nin stands forth in his eminent enlightenment and has routed heretics and demons."

After the two disciples returned to Japan, Nōnin's fame spread far and wide. His chief disciple Kakuan received his sanction and propagated Zen at a temple in Tōnomine in Yamato. One of Kakuan's long-time disciples was Koun Ejō of Eiheiji temple. As Kakuan's death approached, he urged Ejō to go to study with Dōgen. Kakuan handed down to Ejō his compilation of the essential teachings and the personal items he had received from his master Nōnin. When Dōgen saw Kakuan's writings he said in admiration, "Kakuan was indeed a man of clear insight."

One night Kagekiyo came to visit Nōnin. Rejoicing at the unexpected opportunity to meet his nephew, Nōnin sent a disciple to the store to buy wine. But Kagekiyo, suspecting that the officials were being informed of his presence, thrust with his sword and cut his uncle to death. Further details can be found in other sources.[2]

Nōnin's teaching seems to have been a simple one. Special veneration was paid to Bodhidharma, first patriarch of the Zen school, and "a separate transmission outside the scriptures" was championed as the essence of Zen. Nōnin denied the need to engage in customary Buddhist practices or observe the precepts. He further claimed that rewards and blessings are obtainable in the present life.

It is not surprising that Eisai, on his return from his second trip to China, should have been outraged to find a kind of Zen being promulgated in the Kinki area that ran counter to the Zen he had learned abroad and that, moreover, openly made light of the precepts. Recent research has shown that the work for which Eisai is most famous, the *Propagation of Zen in Defense of the Country* (*Kōzen gokokuron*), was in part an attack on the teachings of Nōnin. Eisai argued that the precepts must be maintained and that pure Zen (not the "separate transmission outside the scriptures" version) must be practiced. In this text someone questions Eisai as follows:

> Some people recklessly refer to the Daruma sect as the Zen school. But these [Daruma adherents] say, "There are no precepts to follow, no practices to engage in. From the outset there are no passions; from the beginning we are enlightened. Therefore we do not practice, do not follow precepts. We eat when we are hungry, rest when we are tired. Why recite the Buddha's name, why make offerings, why give vegetarian feasts, why curtail eating?" How can this be?[3]

Eisai replies that the adherents of the Nihon Daruma sect are similar to those people described in the sutras as having a false view of emptiness; they must be avoided at all costs.

Nōnin and his disciples apparently won a considerable following, with temples in Settsu, Kyoto, Tōnomine, and at Hajakuji in remote Echizen. But by the third decade of the thirteenth century, militant monks from Mount Hiei and Kōfukuji temple had destroyed all Daruma temples other than Hajakuji, where most of Nōnin's remaining descendants took refuge.

Philip Yampolsky

Dōgen and Sōtō Zen

Dōgen, the founder of the Sōtō sect, is today the best-known figure in Japanese Zen. He is honored as a religious genius and praised for the depth and originality of his philosophic insight. Of noble descent, Dōgen received a thorough literary education. His parents died while he was still young; following his mother's wishes, he entered the Tendai establishment on Mount Hiei at the age of twelve. When he became dissatisfied with the teachings he found there, he turned to Zen and sought Eisai's guidance at Kenninji temple. It is doubtful that Dōgen ever met Eisai; however, he did study under Eisai's disciple Myōzen (1185–1225). In 1223 he accompanied Myōzen to China, where he visited a number of teachers of the Lin-chi (Rinzai) sect, seeking a master with whom he might feel compatible. Just as he was about to abandon his quest in disappointment he encountered the abbot T'ien-t'ung Ju-ching (Tendō Nyojō, 1163–1228), with whom he established an immediate rapport.

After gaining Ju-ching's sanction, Dōgen returned in 1227 to Kyoto and Kenninji. Displeased by Kenninji's mixture of Zen and esoteric practice, and feeling the pressure of the antagonistic monks of Mount Hiei, he moved to Fukakusa, south of Kyoto, where he established Kōshōji temple. There he taught a strict form of Sung Zen, claiming that proper Zen training required the guidance of a "clear-minded master who has attained the Way." Dōgen wrote:

> I personally saw in great Sung China Zen monasteries in many areas, each built to include a meditation hall, wherein from five or six hundred to one or two thousand monks were housed and encouraged to devote themselves to zazen day and night. The abbots of these monasteries, teachers who transmit the seal of the Buddha-mind, told me when I asked for the essence of Buddhism that practice and realization are not two stages.
>
> For this reason, I urge not only the practicers who come to me,

> but those of high ability who seek the Dharma and those who desire the truth in the Buddha-Dharma, without choosing between beginner and experienced practicer, without taking into account whether someone is enlightened or not . . . to follow the Way of the masters of Zen and to negotiate the Way in zazen.[4]

Dōgen did not attract many disciples, and almost all who came to him had belonged to the controversial sect of Dainichi Nōnin. They included Koun Ejō (1198–1280), who joined Dōgen in 1234, and four monks from Hajakuji in Echizen: Ekan (d. 1251), Tettsū Gikai (1213–1302), Gien (d. 1314), and Chi-yüan (Jakuen, 1207–1299). In 1243 Dōgen abruptly turned over Kōshōji to an obscure disciple and set out for Echizen in north-central Japan. Exactly why he left has not been determined; perhaps it was because of rivalry with Tōfukuji, a nearby Rinzai Zen temple. The area in Echizen to which Dōgen moved was a center of Hakusan Tendai, a mountain ascetic group that had given shelter to many of the Daruma sect disciples who later became Dōgen's own disciples. Dōgen established himself at Eiheiji temple, but his poor health soon led him to hand over his temple duties to his senior student Koun Ejō.

At Eiheiji Dōgen concentrated his efforts on finishing the *Treasury of the True Dharma Eye* (*Shōbōgenzō*), the monumental work on which much of his fame rests. This text consists of ninety-five chapters in its modern recension, about half of them written before the move to Eiheiji. Coincident with this move the tone of Dōgen's writing changed. Where he had praised laypeople's Zen he now attacked it. Where he had refrained from sectarian distinctions he now championed the Sōtō sect and censured Rinzai Zen, claiming that his teacher's lineage (and therefore his own) was the only true Zen. He attacked in scathing terms a major Sung master, Ta-hui Tsung-kao (Daie Sōkō, 1089–1163), and he singled out for particular scorn Te-kuang, the Chinese master who had sanctioned Dainichi Nōnin from abroad. Followers of the Rinzai sect did not respond to these attacks because they were quite unaware of them—the *Treasury of the True Dharma Eye* was kept secret until the first decade of the nineteenth century (and some chapters even remained unpublished until the present century).

With Dōgen's death in 1253, Ejō took over the guidance of the community. Another of Dōgen's disciples, Gikai, had previously inherited the Nihon Daruma lineage from Ekan. Thus two lineages—Dōgen's and Nōnin's—were present simultaneously at Eiheiji. Dōgen's awareness of this developing situation may have been a motivation for his attacks on the Rinzai sect, which had granted Nōnin's credentials. Gikai was sent to various temples in Kyoto and Kamakura and then on to China before succeeding Ejō at Eiheiji in 1267. He attempted to strengthen the temple's ties with the populace by accommodating local deities and incorporating elements of esoteric Buddhism. But an opposing faction of monks, led by Gien and Chi-yüan, protested that such policies violated the strict style of Zen that Dōgen had brought from China. After a five-year dispute, Gikai and his followers abandoned Eiheiji for Daijōji, a former Tendai temple in Kaga. Eiheiji soon fell into decline and virtually ceased to exist for several centuries; during this time the two Sōtō factions remained apart.

Meanwhile, Gikai's heir Keizan Jōkin (1268–1325), often called the second patriarch of Sōtō Zen, established temples throughout the Kaga and Noto areas, trained many disciples, and spread the teaching widely. Following Gikai's lead, Keizan incorporated popular veneration of the bodhisattva Kannon, worship of Shinto deities, and ascetic Shugendō practices into temple ritual.

Sōtō soon became one of the largest sects of Buddhism in Japan. Its priests attended to such needs as the building of roads and irrigation canals, the curing of diseases, and the extirpation of evil spirits. Until about the middle of the Muromachi period (1338–1573), a fairly strict monastic training was maintained. In later years, however, the practice of *sanzen* (interviews with Zen masters) deteriorated, and koan answer books circulated widely. While sanzen training declined, general assemblies (*gokōe*) and meetings for receiving the Buddhist precepts (*jūkaie*) flourished. General assemblies were originally designed to assist in the practice of meditation, and at times as many as a thousand monks participated together. After the mid-fifteenth century, the public was allowed to attend. These events were used to raise funds for the restoration or maintenance of a temple and to impart a general knowledge of Zen to lay parishioners. For the precept ceremonies, a temple would invite a famous priest or precept master to confer the precepts on all classes of people, from feudal lord to commoner. Since these rituals involved several hundred people at a time they were also effective educational and promotional activities.

Early Rinzai Zen and the Rise of the Gozan

The thirteenth and fourteenth centuries saw the flourishing of Rinzai Zen in Kyoto and Kamakura. Some of the Japanese monks who visited China came from Tendai or Shingon backgrounds; on their return they advocated a Zen containing elements of esoteric Buddhism. Others came back with a knowledge of strict Sung-style koan Zen. The Chinese monks who arrived in Japan, refugees from the Mongol conquerors, were often steeped in the literary traditions associated with Sung Zen. Because of the difficulty of communication in a foreign language, they frequently carried on their instruction in writing, further strengthening the literary orientation of the tradition they represented. The steady patronage of the imperial court and the shogunate enabled the medieval Rinzai institution to withstand the opposition of the established schools of Buddhism.

Prominent among the early transmitters of Rinzai Zen was Enni Bennen (Shōitsu Kokushi, 1202–1280). Enni first studied under Eisai's successor Eichō (d. 1247) and several Tendai masters, and he received the Tendai esoteric transmission. Going to Sung China in 1235, he trained under a famous Ch'an master,

Wu-chun Shih-pan (Mujun Shihan, 1178–1249), and became one of Wu-chun's heirs. Enni returned to Japan in 1241, bringing with him over a thousand books dealing with Buddhism and Confucianism. He founded three Zen temples in Kyushu but was attacked by the established schools. After gaining the support of Kujō Michiie (1193–1252), Enni moved to Kyoto and was installed as the founder of Tōfukuji, a great temple complex close to Dōgen's small temple. Enni's teachings emphasized Zen but included elements of esoteric Buddhism.

Another early Rinzai monk, Shinchi Kakushin (Hottō Kokushi, 1207–1298), trained first in the Shingon tradition before entering Zen. Reaching China in 1249, he inherited the teaching of Wu-men Hui-kai (Mumon Ekai, 1185–1260), compiler of the koan collection known as the *Gateless Barrier* (*Wu-men-kuan*). Returning in 1254, Kakushin established a temple in Wakayama. He was frequently summoned to Kyoto by imperial command to lecture on Zen.

Lan-ch'i Tao-lung (Rankei Dōryū, 1213–1278), an emigré Chinese master, arrived in Japan in 1246 with a group of fellow monks. Japan's warrior-ruler, Hōjō Tokiyori (1227–1263), invited him to Kamakura, where he was installed as the first abbot of Kenchōji temple in 1253. Lan-ch'i's Sung-style Zen was devoid of esoteric elements, and he stressed strict observance of the monastic rules:

> The practice of Zen and the pursuit of the Way is nothing other than grappling with the great problem of birth and death. Even on bath days or holidays do not allow your practice of Zen to relax for an instant.[5]

Lan-ch'i made frequent moves: in 1259 he was called to Kenninji in Kyoto; two years later he was called back to Kamakura; and he was twice exiled to the provinces because of slanders by displeased followers. Lan-ch'i spent some thirty-three years in Japan and was one of the principal contributors to Zen's establishment as an independent school.

Beginning in 1338, the new Ashikaga government set up official Zen temples in the sixty-six provinces. Called Ankokuji, these temples were designed to emphasize the political presence of the Ashikaga rulers and lend importance to the provincial lords. Pagodas known as Rishōtō were also set up in the provinces. Dedicated to the spirits of warriors who had died since 1331, these pagodas were located within the precincts of Tendai, Shingon, and Ritsu temples. Here the Ashikaga were directly following a Chinese model, for the Sung government had similarly established official Zen temples throughout the country.

The Japanese Gozan (or "Five Mountains") system developed in the early fourteenth century, following another Chinese precedent. The major temples of Kamakura and Kyoto (soon exceeding the traditional "five") were assigned specific ranks. These rankings were often disputed and frequently revised on the basis of shogunal preference or the influence of important priests; new temples might suddenly be given a rank and older temples dropped. Just below the top-ranked temples were the Jissetsu, or "Ten Temples," located in the provinces. Again the original concept of ten temples was soon abandoned, and some sixty temples were eventually assigned this rank.

When the Ashikaga shogunate was first established in 1338, officials were assigned to supervise the major temples of all schools of Buddhism throughout the country. Since the Ashikaga family had close connections to Zen, they assigned special officials (often with military backgrounds) to oversee the affairs of the Zen institution. As the Ashikaga consolidated their power they turned control over to the Zen priests themselves. Eventually the position of *sōroku* monitored all Gozan Zen affairs: the appointment of chief priests, promotions in rank, ceremonial procedures, and the preparation of documents relating to trade and foreign affairs.

Many famous masters were associated with the Gozan, celebrated as much for their literary accomplishments as their spiritual qualities. Perhaps the best known was Musō Soseki (1275–1351), who at the height of his career had free access to both the court and the shogunate. Descended from an aristocratic family, Musō became a monk at an early age, studying the Buddhist scriptures as well as Confucian and Taoist texts. He received the precepts at Tōdaiji in Nara but soon turned to Zen, visiting numerous teachers in Kyoto and Kamakura. Eventually he came to Kōhō Kennichi (1241–1316), who attempted (without immediate success) to lead him away from a reliance on scriptural and literary works. Musō left Kōhō and spent many years in isolation before gaining his master's sanction.

To a large extent Musō set the style for all the Gozan temples, where literary endeavors and political activity eventually took precedence over traditional meditative practice. He appears to have advocated an accommodation between Zen and the doctrinal schools of Buddhism, as seen in the following passage:

> The Buddha did not call himself only a man of doctrine, nor did he call himself only a man of Zen. Nor did he separate his teachings into a doctrine portion and a Zen portion, because Buddha's inner realization cannot be equated with either of them. The differences between Zen and doctrine come about when this inner realization mysteriously functions to accord with the needs of disciples. . . .
>
> The fundamental intention of genuine doctrinal school masters is thus not bounded by doctrine, and the fundamental intention of clear-eyed Zen masters is not found within Zen. Yet these masters must adjust their speech to their listeners in order to teach.[6]

This position drew criticism from other Zen figures. According to one report, the Daitokuji master Daitō Kokushi (Shūhō Myōchō, 1282–1337) claimed that Musō's understanding remained at the level of the doctrinal schools and that Zen would be ruined if a man of Musō's caliber were to become abbot of an important temple.

The Ōtōkan Lineage

In addition to the Gozan temples, there were other Rinzai Zen establishments in Kyoto that upheld a strict koan Zen and excluded other forms of Buddhism. The principal temples in this group were Daitokuji, which for a while was included in the Gozan, and Myōshinji. The Zen taught at these temples came to be known as the Ōtōkan lineage, after the names of its first three masters: Daiō Kokushi, Daitō Kokushi, and *Kan*zan Egen. Though this type of Zen later suffered to some degree from the literary emphasis and formalization that afflicted the Gozan temples, it has dominated Rinzai Zen from the seventeenth century to the present.

The line was founded by Daiō Kokushi (Nampo Jōmyō, 1235–1308), who began his studies in Japan under Lan-ch'i Tao-lung. In 1259 Daiō went to China and trained under Hsü-t'ang Chih-yü (Kidō Chigu, 1185–1269), who was closely connected with the imperial court. Receiving Hsü-t'ang's sanction, he returned to his former master in Kamakura and then went on to Kyushu, where he taught for three decades. In his final years he was called to Kamakura by the Hōjō regents and installed as chief abbot of Kenchōji.

Daiō's heir was Daitō, who never went to China but nevertheless maintained the strict style introduced by his teacher. Daitō was perhaps the first to establish a systematic program of koan study in Japan. After completing his monastic training he spent some twenty years in relative isolation before emerging as a teacher. Daitō founded Daitokuji and developed a close association with Emperors Hanazono and Godaigo. His rejection of Musō's Gozan-style Zen was noted above. Daitō was succeeded at Daitokuji by Tettō Gikō (1295–1369), who enlarged the temple compound and established branch temples in the wider Kyoto area.

Daitokuji had briefly been assigned Gozan rank by Emperor Godaigo in 1333. When the other Gozan temples protested, ostensibly because Daitokuji had an exclusive method of designating abbotship, the appointment was withdrawn. In 1386 Daitokuji was assigned the lowest rank among the Jissetsu temples, and in 1431 its connections with the Gozan system were completely severed. However, the temple began to regain prominence under Yōsō Sōi (1379–1458) and Ikkyū Sōjun (1394–1481).

Ikkyū is renowned in history and legend for his eccentricities. He was the son of Emperor Gokomatsu, but his mother was forced to leave the court before his birth, so he never attained imperial status. He became a Buddhist acolyte at five and devoted himself to study, displaying an aptitude for Chinese poetry. At twenty he went to Daitokuji to practice Zen. It is said that he was in a boat meditating when he heard crows cawing and attained enlightenment. Ikkyū persistently contended that the Zen priesthood of his day had become corrupt. He especially vilified his brother monk Yōsō, then head of Daitokuji, for allegedly selling certificates of enlightenment and seducing women within the temple precincts. Though Ikkyū spent the last eight years of his life as abbot of Daitokuji, he rejected many of the formalities of Zen, refusing to accept a certificate of enlightenment or grant one to his disciples. He gained further notoriety by openly frequenting the gay quarters and maintaining close attachments to women. Ikkyū's poetry, entitled the *Crazy Cloud Collection* (*Kyōunshū*), includes verses written for a blind singer named Mori:

> Night after night blind Mori sings to me.
> Two mandarin ducks gossiping under the covers.
> Though we vow to be in the Assembly at Maitreya's Dawn,
> Here, in the former Buddha's home, all is Spring.[7]

Daitokuji was destroyed in 1468 during the Ōnin War, as were most of the temples in Kyoto. Reconstruction was begun five years later with the help of rich merchants from Sakai, a port city near present-day Osaka. In the late Muromachi and Sengoku periods (1490–1600), Daitokuji established branch temples throughout the country, often taking over temples once connected with the Gozan.

At the same time a Rinzai branch centering on the descendants of Kanzan Egen (1277–1360) began to attract many monks who were disenchanted with the sterility of Zen practice at the Gozan temples. Kanzan seems to have been a humble Zen teacher content to live in poverty. Granted land in the western part of Kyoto by Emperor Hanazono, Kanzan had built Myōshinji, originally a sub-temple of Daitokuji. In 1399, the Ashikaga shogunate confiscated all Myōshinji's properties and transferred its buildings elsewhere, because the incumbent abbot was a close associate of a family which had revolted against the government. Around 1432, Nippō Sōshun (1336–1448) began restoring the temple, and his work was continued by a succession of able abbots. The support of local lords throughout the country eventually enabled Myōshinji to gain control over many former Gozan temples and outstrip Daitokuji in influence. The priests of this lineage took pains to adopt local beliefs and to conduct services that catered to the common people. In time, traditional Zen practices were neglected, and the master-disciple encounter became formalized. Records of koan interviews that supplied fixed answers to the koans (*missan-chō*) circulated widely.

Developments in the Tokugawa Era (1603–1868)

The establishment of the Tokugawa shogunate at the start of the seventeenth century brought drastic changes to Japanese Buddhism. The new government issued edicts that effectively regulated most aspects of the religion, such as temple construction, the relationship between main and branch temples, the appointment of abbots, and rules of succession. Moreover, the government's Neo-Confucian orientation stimulated anti-Buddhist polemics. In Zen many serious practitioners were at a loss to know how to proceed, feeling that there were few outstanding teachers left to guide them. The Zen institution was perceived as rigid and even corrupt, with greater emphasis on literature and the arts than on genuine training.

In the middle of the seventeenth century a group of Chinese Zen monks arrived in Japan, presumably exiles from the invading Manchu forces. Prominent among them were Tao-che Chao-yüan (Dōsha Chōgen, d. 1662) and Yin-yüan Lung-ch'i (Ingen Ryūki, 1592–1673). Tao-che settled in Kyushu, where he gained numerous disciples. Yin-yüan is famed for having established the Ōbaku sect in Uji, south of Kyoto. There he taught a form of Zen, popular in Ming China, that included elements from the Pure Land school of Buddhism. Yin-yüan's arrival touched off a wave of reform in the Rinzai and Sōtō sects. As Professor Foulk shows in the following chapter, many elements of the current Zen monastic system date from this era.

In the Sōtō sect distinctions among temple and teaching lines had been neglected; priests assigned to a new temple would simply adopt the lineage of that temple. Gesshū Sōko (1618–1696) and his disciple Manzan Sōhaku (1636–1715) were central figures in a movement to restore Sōtō's authentic lineage. A concentrated effort was made to revive Dōgen's teachings, virtually ignored for several centuries. Though steps were taken to publish Dōgen's *Treasury of the True Dharma Eye*, its printing was banned by the Sōtō authorities until 1796, and even then it was not published in its entirety.

During this period a number of Rinzai monks taught their own individualistic style of Zen. Some were renowned popularizers, such as Takuan Sōhō (1573–1645) and Bankei Yōtaku (1622–1693). Others, such as Gudō Tōshoku (1579–1661), represented what they felt to be the orthodox transmission and resisted any intrusion of Pure Land teachings.

The man most responsible for the revival of Rinzai Zen in the latter part of the Tokugawa era was Hakuin Ekaku (1686–1769), whose continuing influence can be seen in this volume. Hakuin turned back to the strict koan Zen of the Sung period that had been brought to Japan by Daiō in the thirteenth century. To this he added new elements of his own devising, laying the foundation for a systematic course of training. At the same time he put great emphasis on making Buddhism accessible to the general public. Equally competent in classical Chinese literature, Buddhist texts, and popular genres, Hakuin wrote extensively. His vigorous style is evident in the following passage, which extols meditation in the midst of activity:

> Do not say that worldly affairs and pressures of business leave you no time to study Zen under a master, and that the confusions of daily life make it difficult for you to continue your meditation. Everyone must realize that for the true practitioner there are no worldly cares or worries. Supposing a man accidently drops two or three gold coins in a crowded street swarming with people. Does he forget about the money because all eyes are upon him? Does he stop looking for it because it will create a disturbance? Most people will push others out of the way, not resting until they get the money back into their own hands. Are not people who neglect the study of Zen because the press of mundane circumstances is too severe, or stop their meditation because they are troubled by worldly affairs, putting more value on two or three pieces of gold than on the unsurpassed mysterious Way of the Buddhas? A person who concentrates solely on meditation amid the press and worries of everyday life will be like the man who has dropped the gold coins and devotes himself to seeking them. Who will not rejoice in such a person?[8]

Hakuin gained a large following in his own time and became the dominant figure in the history of Japanese Rinzai Zen. Today the masters in all the major monasteries trace their spiritual heritage to him.

When we review the broad sweep of Zen's history in Japan, we see that the two major sects, Sōtō and Rinzai, developed in distinctive ways. Sōtō had a halting start: its founder Dōgen failed to win influential patrons, and his lineage was split by a third-generation dispute. Yet Sōtō was the first Zen sect to gain wide acceptance among the populace, and Dōgen is now regarded as a thinker of international significance. The Rinzai sect enjoyed close ties with Japan's military and aristocratic rulers for several centuries, and it exerted considerable impact on the nation's cultural life. A prolonged decline in the rigor of Rinzai monasticism was reversed in the mid-eighteenth century by the forceful master Hakuin. Today the Zen institution struggles in the face of fresh challenges—Westernization, demographic shifts, the appeal of new religions, and so on. Nonetheless, the spiritual, artistic, and intellectual pursuits of contemporary Japan continue to reflect the enduring influence of the multifaceted Zen tradition.

9. The Zen Institution in Modern Japan

by T. Griffith Foulk

In Japan the major schools of Buddhism are conceived as religious clans or lineages. The members of each school feel related to one another by virtue of their descent from a common spiritual ancestor. Japanese Zen is no exception—it traces its lineage back to the patriarchs Bodhidharma (d. 532?) and Hui-neng (638–713). However, there is no single religious body in Japan that encompasses the entire Zen school. Rather, twenty-two independent organizations consider themselves heirs to the Zen lineage. These groups relate to one another like cousins who accept each other's claims to membership in the extended clan, but who prefer to think of themselves as representing the most direct line of descent.

The basic organizational unit in Zen and other traditional schools of Japanese Buddhism is the temple. A temple registered with the government as a tax-exempt religious body is called a "unitary corporation." Japanese law also recognizes an association of temples as a "comprehensive corporation." Most of the present groupings represent a continuation of the head/branch temple system of the Tokugawa period (1603–1868).

The twenty-two Zen comprehensive corporations are listed in Table 1. The one with by far the greatest number of affiliated temples, clergy, and lay adherents is the Sōtō school. Fifteen identify themselves as branches of the Rinzai school; they bear the names of their respective head temples. The Ōbaku school is a comprehensive corporation comparable to some of the middle-

Table 1. The Zen Institution in Modern Japan (1984)[1]

Denomination	*Temples**		*Monasteries***		*Clergy male*	*Clergy female*	*Adherents*
1) Sōtō	14,718	[6]	26	(5)	15,528	1,177	6,885,381
2) Rinzai: Myōshinji	3,421	[7]	19		3,472	224	847,700
3) Rinzai: Kenchōji	406		1		343	3	239,340
4) Rinzai: Engakuji	209		1		181	2	37,800
5) Rinzai: Nanzenji	428		4	(1)	703	61	147,306
6) Rinzai: Hōkōji	169	[2]	1		172	1	69,420
7) Rinzai: Eigenji	131		1		106	11	15,577
8) Rinzai: Buttsūji	50		1		50	1	100,490
9) Rinzai: Tōfukuji	362		3		319	16	50,000
10) Rinzai: Shōkokuji	99		1		83	7	7,152
11) Rinzai: Kenninji	70		1		76	0	26,150
12) Rinzai: Tenryūji	106		1		90	7	89,700
13) Rinzai: Kōgakuji	61		1		28	0	28,850
14) Rinzai: Daitokuji	199	[1]	2		181	9	52,779
15) Rinzai: Kokutaiji	35		1		33	8	1,680
16) Rinzai: Kōshōji	8		0		8	1	3,219
Rinzai Subtotal	5,754	[10]	38	(1)	5,845	351	1,717,163
17) Ōbaku	460		2		681	75	353,070
18) Ichibata Yakushi Kyōdan	31	[31]	0		61	63	195,783
19) Senshin Kyōdan	0	[2]	0		75	314	61,249
20) Nyoraikyō	68		0		5	63	33,204
21) Isson Kyōdan	0	[3]	0		0	1	1,900
22) Sanbō Kyōdan	6	[6]	0		11	0	2,990
Total	21,037	[58]	66	(6)	22,206	2,044	9,250,740

* brackets [ ] signify facilities other than temples ** parentheses ( ) signify nunneries

sized Rinzai branches. Five Zen organizations (numbers 18 through 22) claim no connection with the Sōtō, Rinzai, or Ōbaku schools. Though very small numbers of temples and clergy are involved, these groups represent recent movements to reform traditional Zen practice.

Head Temples

Zen head temples serve as administrative and/or spiritual centers for a comprehensive corporation. Currently there are eighteen: fifteen for the Rinzai school, one for the Ōbaku school, and two for the Sōtō school. Nearly all the rest of the Zen temples in Japan are branch temples affiliated with one of these eighteen, which have much in common. All of them once functioned as major administrative centers in the Tokugawa head/branch temple system. Today they collect annual fees from their branch temples, regulate the ordination and ranking of their clergy, operate schools and research centers, publish materials for lay followers, and administer social welfare. Zen head temples serve as central meeting places for the priests of their branch temples and for the members of nationwide laymen's associations. They stage large-scale ceremonies, conferences, and banquets.

Today many of these head temples are also major tourist attractions for Japanese and foreign visitors. The Rinzai head temples in Kyoto and Kamakura preserve fine examples of medieval Zen monastery architecture, including Chinese-style gates and halls. Many of their beautiful gardens date from the fifteenth and sixteenth centuries. The Sōtō head temples, Eiheiji and Sōjiji, have no buildings of great antiquity, but they are very popular with tourists nonetheless. They offer glimpses of large medieval-style monasteries that still function in accordance with ancient rules. Tourism is a major source of revenue for many Zen head temples and their sub-temples, although the entrance fees are taken as "donations," not subject to taxation. This practice has brought the Zen (and wider Buddhist) establishment into conflict with the civil authorities in recent years, and the principles involved have been bitterly contested on both sides. Whatever the percentage of visitors who consider themselves faithful lay Buddhists, the practice of traveling to temples and other holy sites is an age-old form of popular devotion in East Asia, so it is difficult to draw a line between "pilgrims" and "tourists."

Many of the principal functions of a head temple are associated with a year-round schedule of ceremonies, and these activities tell us much about contemporary Japanese Zen. Some highlights from the annual ceremonial calendar of Myōshinji, the largest of the Rinzai head temples, are described below and presented in Table 2. Many of these practices are also performed, albeit on a smaller scale, at Zen branch temples.

Table 2. Annual Observances at Myōshinji, a Rinzai Head Temple

Month/Day	*Observance*
1/1–1/3	New Year's Assembly
1/16	Virtuous Month Prayer Assembly
1/18	Abbot's Hall Repentance Assembly
2/7	Founding Abbot's Birthday Assembly
2/15	Buddha's Nirvana Assembly
3/21	Equinox Assembly: Mortuary Hall Offering
4/8–4/12	Sutra-chanting Services for Visiting Parishioners
4/8	Buddha's Birthday Assembly
4/9	Mortuary Hall Offering
4/9–4/10	Rinzai's Memorial Service
4/10	Memorial Service for Deceased Head Priests of Myōshinji Branch Temples
4/11	Mortuary Hall Offering
4/12	General Offering
4/14	Sutra-chanting Services at the Various Stupa Sites
4/15	Retreat-opening Dharma Hall Ceremony
4/29	Emperor's Birthday Service
5/16	Virtuous Month Prayer Assembly
5/18	Abbot's Hall Repentance Assembly
6/18	Main Gate Repentance Assembly

7/14	Services at the Various Stupa Sites
7/15	Retreat-closing Dharma Hall Ceremony
7/15	Bon Festival Assembly: Feeding of the Hungry Ghosts at the Main Gate
8/3	Mortuary Hall Offering
9/16	Virtuous Month Prayer Assembly
9/18	Abbot's Hall Repentance Assembly
9/23	Equinox Assembly: Mortuary Hall Offering
10/4–10/5	Bodhidharma's Memorial Service
11/10–11/1	Emperor Hanazono's Memorial Service
12/8	Buddha's Enlightenment Assembly
12/14	Winter Night Services at the Various Stupa Sites
12/25	Year-end Prayer Assembly

The New Year observances at Myōshinji and other Zen temples feature petitionary prayer assemblies. These are intended to forestall calamities and promote benefits in the coming year. Prayer assemblies in Zen include the "revolving reading" of the *Great Perfection of Wisdom Sutra* in six hundred fascicles, by rapidly flipping through the pages without actually reading them. In the monks' hall, the trainees enjoy a feast of *toshi-koshi soba*, which might be translated as "wrap-up-the-year noodles." Several rounds of *zazen* then continue past midnight—the monks enter the New Year in silent meditation.

The three Buddha assemblies commemorate three major events in the life of Shakyamuni Buddha: his birth, his enlightenment, and his entry into Nirvana (death). As shown in Table 2, the traditional dates for these events are April 8, December 8, and February 15, respectively. Offerings and the recitation of formulaic verses form the core of all three ceremonies. Where there are monks in training, the enlightenment assembly is customarily preceded by an all-night meditation session. For the Nirvana assembly a large and ornate scroll that depicts the scene of the Buddha's passing is usually displayed.

Memorial services are rituals in which offerings are made to ancestral spirits on the anniversary (annual or monthly) of their day of death. These spirits are represented by images or mortuary tablets which are placed on an altar. Buddhist sutras and spells are chanted as a device to generate spiritual "merit," which is then offered to the ancestors, together with certain prayers for their well-being. The prayers may differ according to the spiritual rank of the recipients. This "offering of nourishment" also has a quasi-material component: incense is burned while food and drink are placed on the altar. The ancestral figures venerated at Myōshinji are: Bodhidharma, the First Patriarch of the Zen lineage; Rinzai Gigen (Lin-chi I-hsüan, d. 867), the founding patriarch of the Rinzai lineage; Kanzan Egen (1277–1360), the founding abbot of Myōshinji, and Emperor Hanazono (1297–1348), the patron who originally had Myōshinji built. The ancestors of Myōshinji's current patrons, whose family tablets are arrayed on altars in a mortuary hall, are also the recipients of offerings.

Other Zen temples venerate different sets of ancestral teachers, founding abbots, and patrons, but the contents of their memorial services are otherwise the same. The ceremonies for the Zen school's spiritual ancestors differ little from those performed for deceased lay followers. In order to satisfy the ritual requirements of the service, the patriarchal figures worshiped in Zen are assigned precise death days.

According to popular belief in Japan, the midsummer Bon festival and the vernal and autumnal equinoxes are the times when ancestral spirits "return" to commune with the living. The Bon and equinox ceremonies performed by Buddhist priests are directed to the deceased relatives of lay followers and to "all the spirits in the three realms" of existence, especially the so-called hungry ghosts. The nourishment of all the ghosts and nameless spirits who have no relatives to care for them is regarded as an expression of universal compassion, a central ideal of Mahayana Buddhism. On the level of folk religion, such practices can also be understood as a means of propitiating these unstable spirits and thereby preventing calamities.

Fortnightly chanting services are held for the reigning emperor on the first and fifteenth of every month. They resemble the memorial services described above, though in this case the merit is dedicated directly to the emperor. He is represented by a tablet inscribed with prayers for his prosperity; it rests on the central altar below an image of the chief object of worship, Shakyamuni Buddha. The ceremony for the emperor is always followed by sutra-chanting services for the tutelary deities, the ancestral teachers, the god of fire (Katoku Seikun), and the protecting deity of the kitchen (Idaten). The concern for the emperor's well-being stems more from a desire to remain true to the ritual procedures outlined in Sung Chinese and medieval Japanese Zen monastic codes than from any current ideological or political considerations.

Monasteries

Japanese Zen monasteries have preserved forms of training that originated centuries earlier in China and Japan. In the monastery monks (or nuns) lead a cloistered, communal life in accordance with strict rules and schedules, under the guidance of one or more senior teachers. The rigorous training includes zazen, *kōan* practice (in Rinzai and Ōbaku Zen), the study of Buddhist scriptures and Zen classics (more in Sōtō Zen), manual labor, and public alms-gathering. Ancient ritual procedures for etiquette, dress, eating, bathing, and going to the toilet are still observed.

Most Zen monasteries in Japan have a main ceremonial hall and a kitchen-cum-living quarters where the administrative officers have their rooms. Monasteries also have a third major structure that is used by the monks as a dormitory, meditation hall, and sometimes as a place to take meals. In Sōtō this building is called the Sangha hall (*sōdō*) and is based on Sung Chinese models. In Rinzai it is called the meditation hall (*zendō*) and is based on Ming Chinese models introduced into Japan in the seventeenth century. The basic furnishings in both halls are long, low, wooden platforms separated by aisles. Each trainee is assigned a single location on a platform, and there he does zazen, takes formal meals (in Sōtō), and sleeps at night, all in the close company of his fellows. The Sangha halls and meditation halls are also the scene of regular sutra-chanting services and various other rituals, and sometimes they are also used for lectures.

The Sōtō school now has thirty-one monasteries, including five nunneries. The two head temples, Eiheiji and Sōjiji, each have more than one hundred monks in residence at any given time. The monks train under the supervision of the abbot and approximately thirty monastic officers, most of whom are accorded the honorific title of *rōshi* or "venerable teacher." Sōtō monasteries located in branch temples generally have about fifteen monks and one to four senior officers (all addressed as roshi).

The Rinzai school has thirty-nine monasteries, including one nunnery. Most of the major Rinzai organizations have at least one monastery located on the grounds of the head temple. Myōshinji, Nanzenji, and Daitokuji also have a number of separately located branch-temple monasteries (see Table 1). The larger monasteries average twenty-five monks in training at any one time, and the smaller ones have as few as two or three. Whereas Sōtō monasteries bring in priests to serve temporarily as senior officers, all of the administrative and leadership positions in the Rinzai monasteries are manned by the young monks themselves. The one exception is the position of abbot, which is held permanently by a Rinzai Zen master. He is the spiritual preceptor of all the monks, the only person accorded the title of roshi.

The Ōbaku school has its head-temple monastery Manpukuji and one branch-temple monastery. At present Manpukuji has several senior officers and a handful of monks who undergo Rinzai-style koan training. Manpukuji was founded in 1661 by Yin-yüan Lung-ch'i (Ingen Ryūki, 1592–1673), an eminent Chinese Zen master in the Lin-chi (Rinzai) line. Yin-yüan's brand of Zen monasticism stressed observance of the traditional Buddhist rules for monks (*Vinaya*), study of the Buddhist canon, and a combination of Zen and Pure Land practices. His Ōbaku school initially attracted many Japanese Zen monks who were disenchanted with what they saw as the degenerate state of Sōtō and Rinzai. Although in the long run it did not succeed in supersed-

ing those older schools, Ōbaku Zen provoked a spirited reaction from them, stimulating reexamination and reform. Many aspects of monastery training found today in Rinzai and Sōtō reflect Tokugawa period responses to the Ōbaku school.

At the same time, Sōtō and Rinzai scholar-monks began to study medieval Japanese Zen monasticism in an attempt to revive forms of practice once prevalent in their own traditions. By the end of the Tokugawa period, this effort had led to the reconstruction of medieval-style monasteries at Eiheiji, Sōjiji, and a number of lower-echelon Sōtō head temples. In Rinzai Zen, the head temples steadfastly resisted such changes, and reforms were carried out chiefly in new branch-temple monasteries, many of which were supported by regional lords. The followers of Hakuin Ekaku (1686–1769) tried to purge the elements of Ōbaku Zen that they found objectionable. They suppressed the Pure Land practice of reciting Amida Buddha's name, deemphasized the Vinaya, and replaced sutra study with a more narrow focus on traditional koan collections. Even so, many of the forms of monastery organization and lifestyle that had been borrowed from Ōbaku Zen, such as the arrangement of the meditation hall and the taking of meals in a separate dining hall, were retained in the Rinzai branch-temple monasteries.

The total number of Zen monasteries in Japan today, seventy-two, seems small when compared with the more than twenty thousand ordinary Zen temples. Moreover, the number of monks in monastic training at any one time, never more than a thousand even by the most generous estimate, comprises less than five percent of the total Zen clergy (see Table 1). For most monks a monastery is only a temporary step, albeit a very important one, on the road to a lifelong career as the head priest of a temple. Today all but a few monks are the sons (usually the eldest sons) of temple priests, and they are expected to inherit the positions held by their fathers. After college they undergo a minimum period of monastic training, between six months and three years, in order to qualify as the assistant priest of their home temple. In the monasteries they acquire the working knowledge of ritual procedures essential to their professional careers as priests.

The rigorous communal training that takes place in Zen monasteries is very much geared toward the monks, and efforts are made to screen them from the distractions of the surrounding secular society. Nevertheless, there is a tradition in Japanese Zen of allowing serious lay practitioners to train alongside the monks, at least to the extent that the layperson's commitments permit. It is not unusual for the abbot of a Rinzai monastery to have several lay disciples who have trained with him longer (and advanced further) than most of the monks under his tutelage. As far as spiritual development is concerned, Japanese Zen teachers recognize that there are individual differences of potential and attainment that are more significant than the formal distinction between monk and layperson. Lay practitioners in Zen monasteries are not, however, included in those aspects of the training that prepare the monks for their careers as priests. Nor are laypeople allowed to hold any monastic offices or serve others in a priestly capacity.

Insofar as Zen monasteries are places where the average priest gets his basic training, they bear some resemblance in function to theological seminaries in the West. The similarity ends there, however, for monasteries are regarded within the Japanese Zen establishment as institutions that epitomize the Zen life and its values. Communal monastic discipline is the ancient cornerstone of the Buddhist tradition, and it remains the ideal in Japanese Zen today, even if the number of clergy actually involved is small.

The Training of Zen Monks

The training routine is similar in all Zen monasteries. Table 3 details the daily schedule at Zuiōji, a middle-sized Sōtō monastery that enjoys a reputation for strictness and high standards.

Table 3. Daily Schedule at Zuiōji, a Sōtō Monastery

Hour	*Activity*
4:00 a.m.	Bell for rising
4:15	Abbot's incense offering in the various halls*
4:20	Dawn meditation
5:10	Morning sutra-chanting service
6:00	Private sutra-chanting for one's own teachers*
	Service for Idaten (tutelary deity of the kitchen/offices)*
6:20	Morning gruel
7:00	Cleaning
7:40	Morning gathering
9:00	Dharma lecture or scriptural study or manual labor or alms-gathering
10:00	Meditation or manual labor or alms-gathering
11:10	Midday sutra-chanting service
11:30	Midday meal
12:00 p.m.	Free time
1:10	Manual labor
4:00	Seated meditation or continuation of manual labor
4:30	Evening sutra-chanting service
5:00	Evening meal
5:30	Bath
6:30	Free time
7:30	Evening meditation
9:00	Sleep

*activities performed or attended by a few officers only

The principal daily activities of the monks are: manual labor and cleaning; lectures and study; sutra-chanting services; and seated meditation. Another important daily activity, though not listed in Zuiōji's schedule, is individual instruction by senior Zen teachers.

The idea has often been expressed in the Zen tradition that spiritual cultivation should not be restricted to conventionally "religious" forms but pursued in the midst of everyday activities as well. From the awakened point of view, the distinction betweeen sacred and profane is seen as groundless: everything is equally sacred (in Buddhist terms, everything manifests enlightenment), and everything is equally profane (even enlightenment is not some special state). It follows that not only the main ceremony hall and meditation hall, but also the kitchen-administration building, bathhouse, and toilet are understood as places for religious practice. All of these facilities have altars where sacred images are enshrined and offerings made. Moreover, most "ordinary" activities such as eating, bathing, washing the face, and going to the toilet are rendered sacred in Zen monastery life by detailed rules of etiquette and ritual procedure. The procedure for bathing, for example, requires a monk to offer incense and make prostrations at the altar of the tutelary deity of the bath (the bodhisattva Baddabara) before undressing in the prescribed manner. In Sōtō monasteries a verse is also chanted before washing: "In cleansing the body, I pray that the bodies and minds of all living beings shall be without dirt, becoming bright and pure inside and out."

The etiquette for handling one's bowls and utensils at mealtime is highly refined, and prayers are chanted which lend explicit religious significance to the meal. Before the monks eat, they raise their bowls over their heads in a gesture of respectful offering, and they chant:

> The first portion is offered to the Three Treasures [Buddha, Dharma, and Sangha]. The middle portion is offered to the Four Benefactors [parents, nation, teachers, and all living beings]. The final portion is offered to beings in the six paths of rebirth [the realms of gods, fighting titans, human beings, animals, hungry ghosts, and hell]. May they all be nourished.
>
> The first bite is to cut off every evil. The second bite is to cultivate every good. The third bite is to lead all living beings to salvation. May they all attain the Buddha Way!

Though the procedures employed in Sōtō monasteries are usually more complex than those used in Rinzai monasteries, all three schools of Japanese Zen regard strict adherence to etiquette and ritual as a vital aspect of training that fosters mindfulness and builds character. The Sōtō school goes so far as to embrace the maxim: "Etiquette is the Buddha's teaching; ritual propriety is the essential principle of our school."

Manual labor has long been valued in Zen as a form of religious practice. Contrary to the Zen school's own mythology and the claims of some Zen historians, however, manual labor for monks was not the invention of the Zen school in eighth-century China—it was a practice known throughout Chinese Buddhism from as early as the fourth century. Nor is there any solid historical evidence to back up the romantic notion that communities of Zen monks in the T'ang era (618–907) were free from dependence on lay patronage due to their efforts in farming and other forms of labor. In any case, it is certain that the practice of manual labor has little economic significance in Japanese Zen today. Zen monasteries subsist primarily on donations received from the laity. Manual labor is valued chiefly for the lessons it provides in humility and self-reliance, and for the opportunity it affords for practicing "meditation in the midst of action." The latter is conceived as a continuation of the same concentrated state of mind that is cultivated in formal seated meditation. The most common forms of manual labor found in Zen monasteries today are cleaning, vegetable and landscape gardening, pickling vegetables, light maintenance work, and (in some areas) cutting firewood and shoveling snow.

All monks today are at least high school graduates. Many are also graduates of one of the colleges affiliated with the Zen school, where they typically major in Buddhist and Zen studies, a curriculum designed for future Zen priests. There is thus little necessity today for monks to be given the kind of basic academic training that in former times took place in Zen monasteries. Formal group instruction in Rinzai and Ōbaku monasteries is generally limited to lectures (*teishō*) on koans, given by the Zen master. The standard procedure is to work through a collection of koans, commenting on one koan per lecture. Rinzai monks do not engage in any other formal study of Buddhist texts, although they must memorize a number of relatively short scriptures used in sutra chanting. In Sōtō monasteries there is considerably more in the way of textual study, much of it focused on the writings of the Sōtō school patriarchs, Dōgen and Keizan (1268–1325). Besides formal Dharma lectures, there are classroom-style lectures and periods designated for individual study. The Sōtō head-temple monasteries have working replicas of common quarters in the Sung Chinese style. These facilities are outfitted with sitting platforms similar to those in a Sangha hall but used for the study of scriptures rather than meditation (in Sung monastic rules, reading and writing were forbidden in the Sangha hall).

Three daily sutra-chanting services are performed in all Zen monasteries, although the midday and evening services are not always attended by the entire community. The indispensable core of the ritual is the chanting of a verse for the dedication of merit. A good example of such a verse is the one used for abbreviated morning services in Sōtō monasteries and temples:

> We reverently offer the merit just accumulated by chanting the *Heart Sutra* to our great benefactor and lord of the doctrine, the original teacher Shakyamuni Buddha; to the high ancestor Jōyō Daishi; to the great ancestor Jōsai Daishi; to the successive generations of ancestral teachers of the three lands [India, China, and Japan] who transmitted the lamp; to the most reverend (*name*), founding abbot of this temple; to all the succeeding generations of most reverend abbots; and to the eternal Three Treasures in the ten directions. Through this offering may we requite their merciful blessings.
>
> We also make suppliant offerings to the tutelary deity of this temple and to all the Dharma-protecting gods, with prayers that the true Dharma shall flourish, that all nations shall dwell in peace and harmony, that the precincts of this temple shall be tranquil, and that all karmic conditions shall be felicitous.

Since this verse for the dedication of merit belongs to the Sōtō school, it includes offerings to the patriarchs of that school in Japan—Dōgen (Jōyō Daishi) and Keizan (Jōsai Daishi).

The usual daily schedule at most Zen monasteries includes three or four fifty-minute periods of seated meditation. In general, the evening hours are set aside for two or more consecutive sitting periods, interspersed by a few minutes of walking meditation (*kinhin*). There are also periodic meditation sessions (*sesshin*), lasting from three days to a week, during which manual labor is minimized and the hours spent in seated meditation are maximized. Zuiōji, for example, holds one three-day session every month and two week-long sessions annually. Rinzai monasteries generally hold six week-long intensive meditation sessions a year. During sesshin sleep is also sacrificed to increase the time spent meditating. Monks rise even earlier than usual and are urged to continue sitting late into the night. In some monasteries novices are not allowed to lie down at all during their first sesshin.

The instructions for zazen given to beginners are identical in the three main schools of Japanese Zen. Stress is placed on maintaining the correct physical posture, with the legs crossed in the lotus or half lotus position and the back held erect. Meditators are initially taught to focus attention on their breathing as a means of developing mental concentration. Once they have attained some facility in this practice, trainees in Rinzai and Ōbaku monasteries begin koan study under the guidance of the master. The koan replaces the breath as the focus of attention. Ideally, a koan should be kept in mind and investigated in the midst of *all* activities, though the sitting posture is held to be most conducive to concentration. When trainees in Sōtō monasteries are ready to progress beyond the stage of following their breath they are instructed in the practice of "just sitting" (*shikantaza*). In this practice concentration is maintained without focusing the mind on any particular object besides the mind-ground itself.

The question of how zazen and other forms of practice relate to enlightenment or buddhahood is a fundamental issue that divides the Rinzai and Sōtō schools today. The Rinzai teaching is that supreme exertion is needed in order to awaken to the truth that all beings are essentially buddhas. This awakening is called "seeing the nature" (*kenshō*)—that is, seeing Buddha-nature or one's Own Nature. Rinzai masters insist that koan practice is the most efficacious way to attain an initial kensho experience.

Thereafter, they hold, one's insight should be deepened and refined by further koan study until the experience of enlightenment is fully integrated into one's being. The Sōtō position is that because all beings are essentially buddhas, enlightenment manifests itself in seated meditation right from the start, and it should not be conceived as something to be gained in practice. Sōtō teachers stress faith in one's original enlightenment, and they advocate an attitude of nonseeking as the proper frame of mind with which to practice Zen. By adhering to the rules of ritual propriety one is acting like what one already is—a buddha.

In Rinzai and Ōbaku monasteries, there are times during the morning and evening meditation periods when the monks (and laymen, if they have permission) are given the opportunity to rise from their seats in the meditation hall and "enter alone" (*dokusan*) into the master's room. As described in Roshi Kapleau's essay, they make a series of prostrations before the master, recite the particular koan they are investigating, and attempt to satisfy the master that they have penetrated its meaning. When a trainee, sometimes after a long struggle, is able to demonstrate a degree of insight into the koan that meets the master's standards, he is tested with a number of secondary "probing questions" (*sassho*). Finally he is asked to consult a collection of "capping phrases" (*jakugo*) and select one that matches the spirit of the koan. Having succeeded in all of these tasks, he receives a fresh koan to work on. If a disciple progresses steadily in this practice and remains with his master for a sufficient period of time (ten to fifteen years is typical), he may eventually be granted a "seal of approval" (*inka shōmei*) which makes him a Zen master in his own right, qualified to guide others.

Most masters make their disciples work through roughly the same number of koans in roughly the same sequence that they themselves experienced; only then will they grant the seal of approval. However, what transpires between a master and his disciple in the master's room is regarded in Zen circles as something private and sacrosanct, so a master is free to structure the course of koan study in any way that he sees fit. Though the literal meaning of koan is "public case," in fact there are few public standards and little public accountability in the selection of Rinzai and Ōbaku Zen masters.

In Sōtō monasteries the exchange between teacher and student has no predetermined structure. It is common for monks who seek guidance to form close relationships with one or more of the senior officers and to go to their rooms informally for doctrinal or spiritual instruction. Such relationships occasionally result in a monk being granted Dharma transmission (*denbō*) by a monastery teacher. The usual practice, however, is for a Sōtō monk to be given Dharma transmission by the priest who ordained him (in most cases his own father), after he returns from his minimum period of monastery training. Because Dharma transmission is a prerequisite to becoming the head priest of a Sōtō branch temple, virtually all Sōtō priests meet this ritual requirement at a relatively early stage in their careers.

Dharma transmission has a very different meaning in the Rinzai Zen tradition. It takes place when a master grants his seal of approval to a disciple who supposedly has trained closely with him for many years, completed the full course of koan study, and attained a level of understanding that equals—or surpasses—the master's realization. Only a select few qualify; some masters die without acknowledging any spiritual heirs.

Ordinary Temples

The vast majority of Zen temples are ordinary temples, whose chief function is to serve the laity. Lay parishioners are affiliated with ordinary temples as members of "patron households." As may be seen in Table 1, the Zen school as a whole reported more than nine million lay adherents in 1984, based on roughly three million patron households. An average temple serves about one hundred fifty families, although in some instances the number of households may be as low as a dozen or as high as five or six hundred.

Traditionally, the Japanese have looked to Buddhist temples for services relating to death and the care of ancestral spirits. Officiating at funerals and performing regular memorial services for the dead continue to be the foremost duties of a typical Zen priest. Memorial services may be performed either in a temple or in a layperson's home. The priest chants Buddhist sutras and then dedicates the resulting merit as an offering to the person who died, together with formulaic prayers for his or her well-being and eventual enlightenment. There are also offerings of incense, food, and drink. Such ceremonies are probably the most widespread and frequent mode of interaction between the Buddhist clergy and the laity in Japan today. The donations that priests receive when they preside over funeral and memorial services, moreover, provide many Buddhist temples with a substantial portion of their annual income.

Most ordinary temples today are occupied only by a head priest and his family. As we have seen, the son may serve as the father's assistant in performing priestly duties. There is also a system which allows head priests' wives to be formally recognized as religious teachers and to assist in the guidance of the laity. In 1977, half of the Sōtō temple priests' wives (about sixty-five hundred women) had this status. With or without a title, wives are indispensable partners in the daily operation of ordinary Zen temples. They must greet and entertain parishioners whenever the head priest is called away, and they are also in charge of the temple kitchen, where meals for many different occasions are prepared.

Until the Meiji period (1868–1912), marriage was forbidden for most Buddhist clergy by state as well as religious law. (Sometimes female "cooks" or "servants" lived in or near temples and bore the children of priests clandestinely.) Ordinarily, a priest ordained and trained several local boys as young monks in his temple, eventually selecting one of them to be his successor. When the new Meiji government lifted the legal restriction on

marriage, the various branches of the Zen school did not immediately change their rules. It was not until the aftermath of the Second World War, under the influence of American values, that most temple priests began to marry. Increased economic oppor-

tunity and a decline in the social status of the Buddhist priesthood have made temple life less attractive to young men; the few disciples in most ordinary temples today are usually the sons of the head priest.

In rare cases the head priest of an ordinary Zen temple is a nun. In fact, the Zen clergy as a whole has relatively few female members (see Table 1). This pattern is the outcome of a long history of discrimination against nuns in Japanese Zen (as well as in other traditional schools of Japanese Buddhism). It is only in the post-war era that nuns have managed to gain, on paper at least, rights and privileges equal to those of their male counterparts in the Zen establishment. Sōtō nuns, after a long struggle, first won the right to ordain disciples and give Dharma transmission in 1951, and since 1970 they have been allowed to serve as the head priests of low-ranking branch temples. The official status of Japan's Rinzai and Ōbaku nuns lags even further behind that of Sōtō nuns, since their numbers are too small to be influential. Another way in which discrimination has manifested itself, ironically, is in a refusal to accept the propriety of marriage for nuns. Men are granted the privilege of modifying the Buddhist precept that forbids sexual activity for ordained clergy, but women are not. Of course, Zen and other schools of Japanese Buddhism have no monopoly on sexism; it is pandemic in Japanese society.

There is no tradition of regular congregational worship for the laity in Japanese Zen, but it is customary for temple parishioners to gather for certain ceremonies performed by the head priest. The most popular annual observances in ordinary Zen temples are the following:

Observance	*Month/Day*
New Year's Assembly	1/1–1/3
Buddha's Nirvana Assembly	2/15
Equinox Assembly	3/21
Buddha's Birthday Assembly	4/8
Bon Festival Assembly	7/15 (8/15)
Equinox Assembly	9/22
Buddha's Enlightenment Assembly	12/8

The ceremonies held on these occasions are essentially the same as those held at the head temples (compare the above discussion of Myōshinji's annual schedule). The commemoration of the Buddha's birthday, commonly known as the "flower festival," is especially popular at ordinary temples. On this occasion an image of the infant Buddha is set under a canopy of flowers (representing the Lumbini grove where he was born) and bathed with sweetened tea. Sometimes the tea is also drunk by the parishioners, because it is believed by some to have magical properties. At the New Year, parishioners visit their temples to pay respects to the Buddha and other figures. They obtain protective charms written by the priest on strips of paper, which they hang in their homes. In most of these ceremonial activities there is little to distinguish Zen temples from the temples of other Buddhist schools. However, the sermons given at these events by the Zen priests naturally tend to reflect Zen's doctrinal outlook and its approach to practice.

There is relatively little lay involvement in monastery-style training at ordinary Zen temples. A recent survey showed that about six hundred ordinary Zen temples in Japan—less than five percent of the total—have meditation meetings open to the laity on a regular basis. Such meetings are usually held once a week or twice a month. They offer laypeople a taste of the regimen of zazen, sutra-chanting services, and manual labor that Zen monks experience in a monastery. A more popular mode of lay involvement in Zen Buddhist practice is the assembly for giving the Buddhist precepts. These sessions may be held in a single day or run as long as a week. In Sōtō Zen the ceremony involves the following: ritual confession of sin; baptism by water sprinkled on the head; vows of refuge in the Three Treasures; vows to uphold the three comprehensive precepts and ten bodhisattva precepts; and reception of a certificate that establishes the participant in Zen's spiritual lineage.

Seated meditation, koan training, and manual labor are the forms of religious practice that have most often been singled out by scholars as characteristic of the Zen school. Certainly these practices are ones that the Japanese Zen school today values highly and wishes to be known for. However, if we are to judge from observable behavior, no mode of religious expression is of greater concern to Zen Buddhists than rituals in which offerings are made to ancestral spirits. We have seen that memorial services performed for deceased family members are the most common mode of interaction between the Zen clergy and lay devotees. Priests, moreover, perform similar offering services on a daily, monthly, and annual basis for their own set of spiritual ancestors: the line of Zen patriarchs and the successive abbots of a particular temple.

Many aspects of Japanese Zen are not unique to this particular school; similar phenomena are found in other branches of the Buddhist tradition, both in Japan and elsewhere. Concern with the veneration of ancestral spirits is not even unique to Buddhism, but permeates the religions of East Asia. These findings suggest that many of our notions about the "essence" of Zen are due for reexamination. At least in its institutional dimension, Japanese Zen turns out to be much closer to the Buddhist mainstream and much more imbued with Japanese religiosity than its image in the West would lead us to believe.

10. Recent Developments in North American Zen

by Kenneth Kraft

A Japanese Zen master was asked recently to comment on Zen's transmission to a new culture, as in its current transmission to the West. He raised one eyebrow and said, "The first hundred years are the hardest." So far he seems to be right. In the brief history of Zen in North America and Europe, periods of exuberant growth have often been followed by sober retrenchments; promising first steps sometimes turn out to be false starts. But Westerners attracted to Zen have persevered in the face of such difficulties, searching continuously for ways to keep Zen vital in its new cultural contexts. An old Zen adage offers them encouragement:

> Though the bamboo forest is dense,
> Water flows through it freely.

Zen in North America is being transformed by several new developments. Native-born Americans are gaining recognition as the next generation of Zen teachers, setting up centers and accepting students on their own authority. Zen communities are being restructured to meet the changing needs of lay practitioners and/or to clarify the extent of the master's authority. Members of Zen centers are beginning to stress the value of open communication, talking more with each other and with representatives of other religions. We are still too close to most of these developments to see them clearly, much less forecast their outcome, yet the water seems to be finding its way through the forest.

A striking feature of Zen in the West is the simultaneous presence of many historical variants of the tradition. One finds Sōtō and Rinzai lineages from Japan, Sŏn lineages from Korea, Ch'an lineages from Taiwan, and representatives of Vietnamese Zen. This unprecedented diversity is but a piece of a larger mosaic composed of all the Buddhist schools that have been transplanted to the West from Tibet, Thailand, Sri Lanka, China, Japan, and elsewhere. Buddhist traditions from ten different countries were represented at a 1987 conference on "World Buddhism in North America." The resulting mix of terminology, practices, and teaching styles can be bewildering to newcomers and adepts alike.

Though the various Zen communities in North America have their own distinctive backgrounds, most of them have shared certain patterns of development. The late 1960s and early 1970s were boom times: pioneering Zen masters published seminal books, attracted eager students in large numbers, and presided over the creation of major centers. In some cases aspiring members had to be placed on waiting lists. Most of the first-wave practitioners were in their twenties, not yet constrained by careers and families. Clearing country land and gutting city houses, they built dormitories and meditation halls, sewed cushions, and laid out gardens. Many factors contributed to this sudden flowering of Zen in North America: the social freedom of the youthful baby-boom generation; a spiritual malaise exacerbated by the Vietnam War; the exotic but not too alien image of Zen; and the insight and charisma of the first Zen teachers.

From the outset a basic question arose about the nature of Zen training in relation to Zen's popular appeal. Was Zen meant only for the few who could dedicate themselves to an intensive ten- or twenty-year course of training? Or should the teaching be made accessible to as many people as possible, even if that entailed certain compromises of rigor or purity? Steady expansion raised knotty institutional issues as well. Should the Zen master also direct administrative matters? What style of decision-making is appropriate—authoritarian, democratic, or consensual? How are resources to be apportioned among the main community and its distant branches? What happens when a center sponsors or runs a business? These questions are no less urgent today than they were ten or twenty years ago.

At many of the centers rapid development was followed by some kind of internal upheaval. In more than one instance the master's heir-apparent declared his or her independence ahead of schedule and introduced a variant teaching style. In other cases, jarring revelations about the personal conduct of the teacher shattered long-held assumptions and caused prolonged crises. Members struggled to repair the damage, or waited uncertainly, or left Zen entirely. At some centers leadership changed hands after a painful period of disruption; elsewhere the teacher retained his position. The turmoil in several communities has yet to run its course. In the winter of 1983, a member of one troubled center wrote:

> Last spring we became the first new American religious community to effectively tell its leader to stop. It has been painful, but I think that the way the people of Zen Center have faced this crisis could be an encouragement to other religious communities facing similar problems.[1]

In light of the revelations of improper conduct by certain Zen teachers, a question arises as to what degree these disclosures have hurt the nascent Zen movement in the West. Responses vary, though most agree that the damage is not irreparable. Some disillusioned practitioners recall that Zen was initially attractive to them because its representatives were supposed to be living embodiments of the teaching. Others are willing to make a distinction between a Zen master and Zen Buddhism itself, believing that the transgressions of a few individuals do not necessarily reflect upon the tradition as a whole. There are even some who find fault with "idealistic students . . . who confuse the teacher with their own notion of a 'true' spiritual leader."[2] The Watergate episode has been offered as a rough analogy: the president was forced to resign, the presidency was temporarily tarnished, and certain restrictive laws were passed in Watergate's wake, yet Americans did not seriously question the institution of the presidency itself.

Thus Westerners' respect for Zen generally remains intact, though their perceptions of a Zen master's role may have changed. A former resident of a West Coast center reflected:

> A person beginning practice should look at someone's actions rather than at what they say. That is where Zen practice counts. If you are truly practicing, it will show up in your life. The precepts are important—doing good. Are you hurting others? . . . I think that a teacher's job is to be a tool for students to get in touch with their own teacher within. A teacher's job is not to say, "Trust me, I know what is best." That is a major shift in viewpoint for me.[3]

A senior disciple at another center in transition develops this point further:

> In the Orient, every craft has transmission from master to disciple. Its purpose is to protect against unauthorized and self-appointed teachers. But this aggrandizement of transmission in the minds of young meditators has not served our interests. What is being authenticated? Every word and deed for the rest of someone's life? We have an idealized image of an enlightened person. It's not, strictly speaking, accurate to speak of an enlightened person, but rather of enlightened activity.[4]

As it entered the 1980s, North American Zen suffered a recession. Almost all the centers reported drops in membership, financial strains, lowered attendance at workshops and retreats, and difficulty filling staff positions. Several newsletters temporarily suspended publication. Some of the first-generation teachers retired, and others allowed new constraints to be placed on their secular or spiritual authority. Long-time practitioners struggled to squeeze a few precious hours of meditation into lives increasingly complicated by the demands of jobs and families.

The growing pains of American Zen can be attributed to a complex mix of factors. A number of these involve the teachers: some were disoriented by the discrepancies between their monastic backgrounds and the secular settings of their American centers; many were overextended by unwieldy teacher-student ratios; and their sectarian tendencies inhibited meaningful coordination between groups. Greater weight should perhaps be given to external factors: shifting demographic patterns in the general population, the resurgence of Christianity and Judaism in certain quarters, and the conservative *Zeitgeist* of the 1980s. The careerism that drives so many of today's young people leaves little room for such seemingly nonproductive pursuits as Zen practice. In fact, most of the people now attending Zen workshops for the first time are in their thirties and forties, members of the same generation that inaugurated the counterculture of the 1960s. In an age of conservatism and unabashed pursuit of wealth, Zen finds itself swimming against the tide, at times struggling to stay afloat.

Yet signs of another phase are already evident. Like the Japanese *daruma* doll that rights itself each time it is pushed over, North American Zen is beginning to reestablish its center of gravity. For most of those who have survived the previous ups and downs, aspiration and commitment are as deep as ever. In comparison to the 1960s, however, their expectations are perhaps more realistic, and their time-frame is longer. This is also a period of transition and innovation: new teachers, new centers, and new publications continue to appear. In the spring of 1986, Roshi Philip Kapleau announced his first spiritual successors; one became director of the Rochester Zen Center, and two lead Zen centers in Canada. About the same time the San Francisco Zen Center chose a new abbot, giving him the post for exactly four years (a term with a particularly American ring). Beginning in the summer of 1986, second-generation representatives of most of the North American centers have been meeting annually to explore avenues of current and future cooperation.

Lay Practice and the Role of Women

Zen is primarily a monastic tradition in Asia, but in North America it has been developing essentially as a lay movement. Robert Aitken Roshi notes the implications of this transition:

> This change is most striking in centers like my own where no one including the teacher is ordained. We are no longer dependent on a system of religious training. We are no longer living our practice in a formal way full-time. So inevitably this places more responsibility upon us individually to learn what our practice is and to carry it forth.[5]

Such a fundamental shift can only be achieved through persistent experimentation. Two parallel developments can be observed: attempts to establish some kind of indigenous monastic order, and attempts to create means and structures that allow laypeople to practice Zen seriously.

Most of the Zen centers have struggled, at one time or another, to establish a monastic order. Typically, a few highly committed practitioners take additional monastic vows (such as celibacy or poverty), receive a new Buddhist name, shave their heads, don formal robes, and try to live the life of a monk or a nun. In 1978, one of these American Zen monks spoke about his commitment:

> After I was ordained, the Roshi, the Sangha, the teaching were all suddenly different. It was as if they had been taken into my heart in a new way, and I felt a gladness only before experienced after passing my first koan. Why? Perhaps first and foremost because ordination consists of *vows*, lifetime vows that are taken formally, before the members of the Sangha and one's teacher. Having made this step, I felt swallowed up in the ocean of Buddhism stretching back to beginningless time and on into the endless future.
>
> Of course, there are also the trappings—shaving one's head, wearing only black—but these are really more than trappings. They are an ongoing and continuous affirmation of vows and commitment, as well as a "negation," in a sense, of the vanities, attachments, and other personality things that dilute those vows. The trappings not only help one's practice but are a conspicuous declaration of faith to the public.[6]

A newly ordained monk frequently discovered, however, that two essential ingredients were lacking: a real monastery, and a society that appreciated the monastic vocation. An American monk typically continued to serve as an administrator within the same lay Zen community, eventually concluding that little had changed except his definition of himself. Few survived long in this difficult role. Some modified their vows to permit marriage, while others made extensive pilgrimages to Asia to experience their vocation in a more congenial cultural setting (though they encountered other obstacles abroad as foreigners). In one extreme case, a member of the Providence Zen Center gave away all his possessions, was ordained as a monk, and changed his mind three days later.

As the odds against a viable monastic order lengthened, the development of a strong lay practice became all the more imperative. In Western Zen the most pressing question remains: How can laypeople integrate authentic Zen training into their lives? On a very practical level, this issue is one of time. A certain amount of seated meditation each day (say, thirty minutes or an hour) enables a practitioner to maintain a steady rhythm in his or her practice, but for many aspirants such uninterrupted periods are hard to find on a regular basis. It is even more difficult to schedule time off from work or other obligations for intensive training retreats (*sesshin*), which may last four or seven days. Zen centers need the donated labor of their members in order to function, yet many practitioners barely manage to meditate at their centers, much less work there. Zen students inevitably make compromises in some areas and sacrifices in others. A married couple reported, "Because we spent most of our holidays going to sesshin, we did not have a real vacation for nearly a decade." A doctor and mother of three teenagers describes a typical dilemma:

> We have a tremendous yearning to take the spiritual search all the way to the bottom, to put aside all the things that restrict and bind us and keep us from pursuing that search full-time. To do that, we have to do zazen. We have to do retreats, set aside hours, days, weeks to pursue that search. Meanwhile, what are we leaving at home? Jobs, housework, children. As we sit, visions of spiritual orphans float through our heads. We picture our child wandering through the neighborhood, dirty in an unironed shirt, thumb in his mouth. Someone says, "Where's your mommy?" "My mommy is getting enlightened."[7]

The problems are even more pressing for practitioners or teachers who want to work on the staff of a Zen center but who also have a family. At the national gathering of second-generation teachers and senior students in 1987, all but three of the eighteen participants were parents. With undisguised emotion, they asked themselves and each other, "How can I be a good parent and run a Zen center?" It may also be difficult financially for a small center to support a teacher with a spouse or children. Many unique arrangements have resulted. One staff couple hit upon a way to lead the early morning meditation sessions while their eight-year-old daughter slept in their apartment next door: they installed an intercom in the meditation hall so their daughter could buzz them if she woke early. Such ad hoc solutions are part of the indigenization of Zen in North America.

If Western Zen cannot survive as a lay movement it may not survive at all. Thus there is a continuing struggle to establish Zen as a lifetime religious way rather than a narrowly goal-oriented practice. Whereas some Asian Zen masters (such as Dōgen) once argued that only monks can fully realize the Dharma, contemporary Western advocates of Zen counter that the path of a layperson is no less authentic. Canadian Zen teacher Albert Low articulates this position:

> One can, by committing oneself fully to the lay life and the sacrifices that it takes, in other words to live fully and authentically the role of a parent and spouse, be committing oneself fully to awakening, to the Dharma. But such a commitment needs constant work, just as commitment to being a monk needs constant work. It is like steering a ship across the ocean; one cannot lash the tiller and then forget about it. It means constantly checking one's course and correcting direction.[8]

Another significant feature of Zen in the West is the full-fledged participation of women. In most Asian countries Buddhism perpetuated the sexist attitudes of the entire culture, and Zen was no exception. The spiritual lineage of Zen is called the "*patriarchal* line." Eisai, a twelfth-century Zen pioneer in Japan, stressed that "nuns, women, or evil people should on no account be permitted to stay overnight" in a monastery.[9] Only in recent years have Japanese Zen nuns been allowed to ordain disciples or serve as head priests of temples, as Professor Foulk notes in his essay.

In contrast, women have been instrumental in North American Zen since its inception. Men and women sit shoulder to shoulder in the meditation hall, and women are in positions of influence at each of the major Zen centers. Members of the Diamond Sangha in Hawaii publish a journal about women and Zen called *Kahawai*. Several women have now become teachers themselves, consciously exploring ways to exercise spiritual authority without becoming authoritarian. For example, one female teacher eschews the traditional Zen warning stick and instead uses her hands to strike (or even massage) the shoulders of seated meditators. The Providence Zen Center has taken the lead in acknowledging the importance of women in North American Buddhism, through a series of annual conferences. Dr. Joanna Macy, a popular speaker at such events, believes that women have a pivotal role in the future development of the Buddhist tradition:

> As American women opening to the Dharma, we are participating in something beyond our own little scenarios. We find ourselves reclaiming the equality of the sexes in the Buddha-Dharma. We are participating in a balancing of Buddhism that has great historic significance. . . . I see Buddhism as a tradition that has suffered under several thousand years of patriarchy. Now there is a return, and we can see more clearly the male-dominated, hierarchical patterns that have arisen in the last two millenia. . . . We do not have to buy into hierarchical understandings of what power is, because the central teaching of Lord Buddha himself—the vision of dependent co-arising—shows that power is essentially relational and reciprocal.[10]

In the above passage Macy links the equality of the sexes to the social structuring of power, an issue that may pose even a greater challenge to Zen in the West. Zen was nurtured in a cultural context that valued vertical relationships: the person below was supposed to be loyal to the person above, and the person above was supposed to be responsible for the one below. The seniority system in Zen monasteries affects nearly all aspects of monastic life. If one monk arrives in the morning and another arrives that afternoon, the afternoon arrival has to defer to the morning arrival throughout their monastic careers. In contrast, Westerners increasingly expect their religious communities to embody the ideal of egalitarianism. This principle is frequently invoked among the students themselves, and sometimes it is even extended to the teacher-student relationship.

The transition from hierarchy to democracy can be seen in modifications of religious garb. A *rakusu* is a small biblike square of cloth that hangs across the chest, emblematic of Zen monks in Korea and Japan. In the early years of one of the established American Zen centers, no one wore a rakusu except the teacher. Then rakusus were given to those who had completed the first stage of their koan training. Perceived as badges of spiritual attainment, they began to generate subtle forms of "rakusu envy." So the policy was changed, and rakusus were given out equally to anyone who had been a member of the center for at least three years and who had participated in a precept-taking ceremony. Sewing kits were distributed, and the new recipients were expected to make their own rakusus. The most recent amendment is that only one year of membership (plus precept ceremony) is required for a rakusu.

Will Westerners' democratic impulses constrict or compromise the genuine spiritual authority of a Zen master? How will Zen be changed when the female masters exert significant influence? The repercussions of Zen's encounter with feminism and egalitarianism have yet to be played out.

A New Generation of Teachers

Most of the pioneers of Zen in the West came from Japan, Korea, or other Asian countries. Their beginnings were modest, as they typically arrived with little English or financial backing. Shunryu Suzuki (1904–1971) came to San Francisco in 1959 not to teach Zen to Americans but to lead a congregation of middle-class Japanese-Americans. In 1962 Joshu Sasaki began instructing students in a tiny one-bedroom house near Los Angeles; the bedroom became the teaching room, and the garage served as a meditation hall. When the Korean monk Seung Sahn arrived in Providence, Rhode Island in 1972, he started out working twelve hours a day in a Korean-owned laundry. This first generation also included a few Westerners who had gone to Japan for Zen training, persevered there for a decade or more, and returned as teachers. One of them, Philip Kapleau, was still in Japan when his influential book *The Three Pillars of Zen* was published in 1965. The following year he accepted an invitation to lead a small group of spiritual seekers in Rochester, New York; most of the group's members were middle-aged women with no experience of seated meditation. In the late 1960s and early 1970s the pioneer Zen teachers succeeded in founding large centers, often with several hundred local members and an equal number of members elsewhere.

A living Zen master was something new to most Americans, and expectations were high. Telling images of a master are found in an early documentary film about Tassajara, the mountain retreat of the San Francisco Zen Center, then headed by Shunryu Suzuki Roshi. In one scene Suzuki's young American attendant tells the camera:

> One of my jobs is to remove our teacher's tray after his meal. When he eats an apple, he eats it so completely that the remaining core is as thin as a matchstick. A Zen master does everything in a masterly way.[11]

In the early days of American Zen a master was supposed to be a fount of transcendental wisdom, a moral exemplar, a savvy administrator, and a compassionate personal counselor, not to mention a meticulous eater of apples. In short, a master was expected to be enlightened, and enlightenment was often understood to mean perfect in every way. Whereas in Japan and other Buddhist countries familiarity with countless living representatives of the tradition tempered the urge to idealize, in the West authentic teachers were virtually unknown, and misconceptions about the "Zen master" often went unchecked.

As the established Zen centers commemorated their fifteenth or twentieth anniversaries, a new generation of teachers began stepping forward. Inevitably, the heirs of the pioneers differ from their predecessors in several respects. Most of them are native-born Americans trained in American Zen centers. The typical career pattern includes three elements: long years of continuous service on a Zen center staff, a few years as leader of a smaller Zen group affiliated with the main center, and about a year of pilgrimage and/or further religious training in Asia. Today there are relatively more Zen teachers and relatively fewer Zen students than there were fifteen years ago, resulting in smaller student-to-teacher ratios.

As in any other field, the occupant of a new position does not always feel fully prepared. Sensei Bodhin Kjolhede, Roshi Kapleau's successor at the Rochester Zen Center, described his acceptance of the position in the following manner:

> It wasn't a decision, really. I decided nothing. It was more like suddenly finding out you're in a play that now calls for your entrance on stage. You don't know the rest of the script, not even what kind of play it is—tragedy, heroic epic, comedy . . . whatever. But you do know it's time to enter stage. So you do it.[12]

Second-generation teacher Lincoln Rhodes, abbot of the Kwan Um Zen School (Providence Zen Center), candidly explains that his new role involves a certain amount of on-the-job training:

> None of you asked me to be your teacher. I didn't even ask myself to be in this situation. It just happened to us together. It takes time for people to want that and to be able to use that. Maybe they'll decide they don't want to, and that's okay too. It also takes time for the people who are put in the position of being teachers to be able to do it. Just because Soen Sa Nim [Seung Sahn] gives someone permission to teach, it doesn't mean all of a sudden you're a great teacher. By analogy, maybe you can fix your own car, but you've never done Toyotas, and now it's interesting because you *have* to work on all kinds of cars.[13]

As yet North American Zen seems to lack appropriate terminology for a Western Zen teacher. "Zen master" strikes many (including the teachers themselves) as a bit grandiose, especially for men and women around the age of forty. Among the titles in current use are: Roshi, Sensei, Soen Sa Nim, Sunim, Abbot, Spiritual Director, Dharma Teacher, and Master Dharma Teacher. "Roshi" is the Japanese term for a Zen master or senior Zen teacher. "Sensei" is a more general Japanese word for any teacher or doctor. "Soen Sa Nim" (or "Son Sunim") is a Korean term for a Zen master or monk, and "Sunim" designates any Buddhist monk or teacher in Korea. "Abbot" is used by one center to redefine the teacher's role in institutional terms. "Spiritual Director" (or just "Director") identifies a teacher as head of a particular center. A "Master Dharma Teacher" is sanctioned to lead retreats and give formal Zen interviews at one center, while a "Dharma Teacher" at another center is someone who leads introductory workshops. Often the meaning of these expressions remains obscure even in the centers where they are used. Nor is there any coordination of titles among the various groups. A tendency toward semantic inflation has been noted in some Zen communities: though "Master Dharma Teacher" sounds like a venerable and widely acclaimed patriarch, one recent recipient of the title was under thirty-five and another had less than ten years of Zen training.

Increased Interaction and Involvement

Setting up Zen centers where none had existed before was a daunting task, one that fully absorbed the energies of North American Zen during its early years. At some centers this inward focus may have shaded into insularity. But a new sense of openness is evident in these groups, as Zen followers reach out to others who have similar concerns. The second-generation teachers' interest in an effective network of peers has been noted, and the increased interaction between the scholarly and practicing communities is exemplified by this volume.

Zen Buddhists are more frequently in contact with other Western Buddhists. A current Zen student might subscribe to the *Vajradhatu Sun* (newspaper of a North American Buddhist group with Tibetan roots) or listen to the taped talks of American meditation teachers trained in a Southeast Asian Buddhist tradition. *Spring Wind*, a nonsectarian Buddhist journal published by the Zen Lotus Society of Toronto and Ann Arbor, serves a network that it has helped to create. Efforts are also being made to reach out to Buddhists in Asian-American communities, the so-called "ethnic Buddhists." At a Zen center in Toronto, the meditation sessions attract young Westerners, the devotional activities attract Korean grandmothers, and the two groups are said to inspire each other. Also in Toronto a Buddhist Council of twenty-one groups annually coordinates a celebration of the Buddha's birth. This multicultural event attracts wide attention: the mayor sends a representative, and the festivities are televised. In 1985, Buddhists in New York City established a similar pan-Buddhist organization.

Zen adherents also contribute to the ongoing dialogue between Buddhism and Christianity. In the 1960s Thomas Merton wrote: "The truth of the matter is that you can hardly set Christianity and Zen side by side and compare them. This would almost be like trying to compare mathematics and tennis." Yet Merton went on to argue that when these traditions are understood in their "pure state," they can "complement" each other.[14] Today the dialogue continues in several arenas: academics hold conferences; local churches invite Buddhist speakers; young people attracted to Zen explain themselves to their parents. The University of Hawaii organizes conferences on the Christian-Buddhist encounter that have attracted hundreds of scholars and have been supported by the Luce Foundation and the National Endowment for the Humanities. The Naropa Institute in Boulder has sponsored five annual conferences on Christian and Buddhist meditation. Eido Shimano Roshi was a participant in the most recent of these, responding to such questions as, "Are Christ-nature and Buddha-nature two names for the same thing?" Certain representatives of both faiths see great promise in the Christian-Buddhist dialogue:

> It has to be said now that despite all the brilliant developments and technological innovations we have witnessed, the encounter between Buddhism and Christianity is the most significant event of this century.[15]

Another sign of increased involvement is the growing awareness of the social/political realm. More than ever before, Zen students are participating in antinuclear, environmental, sanctuary, and other movements, on both local and national levels. The Vietnam War prompted vigorous responses at several centers, including all-night meditation vigils, memorial services for the war dead, regular fasting, donations to a Vietnamese Buddhist order, and written appeals to public officials. Americans were inspired by the example of Thich Nhat Hanh, a Vietnamese Zen monk working tirelessly for peace in his own country and abroad. A relatively new term, "engaged Buddhism," endorses the actualization of the Buddhist ideals of wisdom and compassion in the social realm. In 1978 Robert Aitken Roshi and some of his Zen students formed the Buddhist Peace Fellowship, which aims to "bring the peace movement to Buddhism, and Buddhism to the peace movement." Increasing numbers of North American Buddhists are seriously exploring the possible connections between Buddhism and nonviolent activism.

A Tradition in Transition

The future shape of Zen in the West (or Buddhism in the West) is difficult to foresee. Inevitably, new forms will continue to appear. Will Zen survive as a discrete religion? Will it join forces with other Buddhist schools? Might a synthesis of Buddhist contemplation and Christian ethics eventually emerge? Will Zen contribute to some "New Age" paradigm that integrates religion and science? Or might Buddhism and Zen shift in a political direction, perhaps in alliance with a nonviolent peace movement? Few will argue that the old wine of Zen should be presented to the West only in old bottles (East Asian cultural forms). Americans often demand the "new, improved" version, even in spiritual matters, and there may be some inclination to distill a new wine and package it in new bottles. But the result might no longer be Zen, nor compare in quality to its predecessor. The appropriate response may be to preserve the old wine, let it age even further, and design effective new bottles for it.

Several lines of development are already evident. In certain Western Zen communities many traditional Asian forms of practice and organization are deliberately maintained; an Asian language is preferred for vows, chants, technical expressions, and the religious names given to disciples. Other centers have consciously sought to assimilate Zen into Western modes of thought and feeling. In Rochester, Roshi Kapleau found the following adaptations to be effective:

> English chanting versions of basic sutras, distinctive Western dress permitting easy crossing of the legs for zazen, Western-sounding Buddhist names for those who became ordained or took the precepts, and ceremonies, forms, and rituals that are in accord with our Western traditions.[16]

Other innovations have been vigorously pursued by Master Seung Sahn at the Providence Zen Center. Despite opposition from his Korean order (which holds monks to celibacy), he created the role of "Bodhisattva monk," a committed practitioner who may marry and pursue a career. Seung Sahn is receptive to future transformations as well:

> When Bodhidharma came to China, he became the First Patriarch of Zen. As the result of a "marriage" between Vipassana-style

> Indian meditation and Chinese Taoism, Zen appeared. Now it has come to the West, and what is already here? Christianity, Judaism, and so forth. When Zen "gets married" to one of these traditions, a new style of Buddhism will appear. Perhaps there will be a woman Matriarch and all Dharma transmission would go only from woman to woman. Why not? So everyone, you must create American Buddhism.[17]

Another variation is offered by Bernard Tetsugen Glassman Sensei, the senior heir of Taizan Maezumi Roshi (Zen Center of Los Angeles). In Glassman's Zen Community of New York, Zen meditation is the central practice, but the meditation hall is nondenominational, and Catholic and Jewish services are observed along with the Zen rituals. Members run a commercial bakery and are actively involved in social service. One of Glassman's stated aims is to make Zen accessible to as many people as possible:

> I saw the importance of spreading the Dharma, the necessity to develop a Dharma training in America that would help many people. . . . I wanted to work with greater numbers because I saw the "crying out" of all of us, even those who do not feel they are crying out.[18]

At an extreme point along the spectrum of adaptation lies a group that has dissociated itself from its Zen origins. Toni Packer, former disciple of Roshi Kapleau and former trustee of the Rochester Zen Center, left that center when she found herself unable to teach within the Buddhist tradition. In 1986 a lingering reference to Zen was removed from the name of her organization, Springwater Center, with the following explanation:

> At that time we still had a number of traditional Zen practices in our format which we have over the years dropped. Still we have been linked in people's minds not only with Buddhism, but also with Japanese traditions. Our work is without any of these ties. . . . [W]henever the work of the organization should be made clear, the phrase "for meditative inquiry and retreats" will be added.[19]

Some of the most time-honored aspects of Zen training will continue to undergo modification. If a Western meditator is unable to assume a cross-legged position, he or she does zazen sitting in a chair or kneeling on a specially designed bench. While sesshins originally required uninterrupted attendance, from the first bell to the last, several American centers are experimenting with arrangements that allow busy lay practitioners to attend only a few days of a week-long sesshin, or even to commute to it. Koan practice will undoubtedly change as well. In Chapter 4, Eido Roshi cited several passages from non-Buddhist sources as suitable for a new koan collection for Westerners. One of his students would add the following "koan" to such a list:

> Ol' man river, dat ol' man river,
> He must know sumpin', but don't say nothin',
> He jus' keeps rollin',
> He keeps on rollin' along.[20]

A master's follow-up questions might include: How long has old man river been rolling along?; Get all of old man river into one shot glass; Turn old man river onto its back; Make old man river flow across the Mojave Desert; "Tote dat barge! Lift dat bale!"; "Git a little drunk an' you land in jail"; and so on.

In earlier eras, whenever a school of Buddhism penetrated a foreign culture, many centuries passed before the process of indigenization ran its course. Some pioneers consciously refrained from tampering with the imported model, believing that a native tradition would arise naturally through sincere practice and the passage of time. We can only speculate about the rate of Zen's future development in the West. Will a new generation of youth embrace Eastern religions? Will the baby-boomers who first explored spiritual alternatives in the 1960s turn again toward these concerns once their careers and their children have matured? Will Zen's absorption be accelerated by modern means of communication, retarded by the secularism of the age, or affected by other factors still unknown? At some point North American Zen may lose its countercultural cast and more fully enter the social mainstream, where it would confront many of the same obstacles that established religions currently face.

Whenever a religion is transmitted to a new culture it is forced to redefine itself. This process is sometimes explicit, sometimes implicit, as new adherents seek to identify the essentials of the foreign tradition and describe their beliefs to others. When Zen (Ch'an) moved from China to Japan in the twelfth to fourteenth centuries, several criteria of authenticity were widely acknowledged; foremost among them were enlightenment and zazen. Yet some of the standards considered indispensable in that era, such as the correct layout of a Zen monastery, are of little concern to contemporary devotees of Zen.

What are the criteria of authentic Zen today? To put the question more concretely: If you are going to a Zen center or meeting a Zen master, what do you look for to reassure yourself that you have found the real thing? The possibilities are diverse: proper institutional affiliation, spotless surfaces and neatly arranged shoes, the master's lifestyle, the strictness of the meditation schedule, a twinkle in the eye, and so on. Samu Sunim, a Korean Zen teacher in North America, treats moral rigor as a criterion of authenticity when he says, "Korean Zen, unlike its Japanese counterpart, has always maintained a strong attitude and discipline in morality as a prerequisite."[21]

Any search for Zen's essentials in the North American context will be a complex process. Several branches and several national variants of Zen are present, each with a distinctive approach to practice. In addition, the demands made of Zen by its Western followers continue to shift in unforeseen ways: a practitioner who once needed many hours of solitary meditation may now want the religion to provide joyous festivals for her children. Cherished beliefs about Zen are also called into question by crises within the Zen communities. In this fluid situation, one criterion alone is usually not enough to settle the matter of authenticity. Each person is compelled to develop his or her own cluster of standards, refining them continuously to reflect new experiences. For the present, the central issue of authenticity can only be left as a question, but perhaps this is as it should be—fixed essences of any kind are consistently challenged in Buddhism.

A Zen master on his deathbed, pressed by his anxious disciples for instructions about the future of the temple and the teaching, simply replied, "The Dharma will take care of itself." If that is so, Zen will eventually find its own way in its new Western setting:

What a beast!
How to rope it no one knows,
For it has neither nose or tail.
Free hangs its halter,
Yet it does not trample
On the fields of seedling rice.
To the sound of a shepherd's flute,
On the home-way it returns,
Meandering through the spring land
Of primordial buddhas.[22]

Epilogue: Problems of Authority in Western Zen

by Martin Collcutt

The transmission of a spiritual tradition to a very different cultural environment is bound to be a long and difficult process. This is especially true for Buddhism and other Asian religions in the West, where these traditions do not have any preexisting roots. When we consider that it took several centuries for Chinese Zen to be introduced and take root in medieval Japan, a society with a common Buddhist cultural context and a shared written language, it is fair to suggest that Zen in the West is still in an early stage of acclimatization. Professor Kraft's account has shown that the Zen boom of the 1960s and early 1970s has passed, and that Western Zen has entered a critical period of maturation and generational transition.

A number of Zen groups in North America have recently experienced severe growing pains. Some have been divided over the most suitable forms of practice for Western students of Zen. Some have suffered because of a confusion of lay and monastic goals, attempting to impose a lifestyle appropriate for a monk or nun on laypeople with regular work and families to consider. Several communities have had to deal with problems of leadership and organization. There have been teachers who have confused their personal interests with those of the community or who let social acclaim go to their heads. There have been one or two who found themselves too poorly trained or too inexperienced to offer the guidance expected of them. Others have behaved arbitrarily, favoring a particular group in the community or refusing their guidance to certain individuals. There have been instances of teachers who have gone beyond the normally accepted teacher-student relationship in Zen, taken advantage of the authority of their office, and imposed their personal sexual desires on male or female students. Most of these problems have been settled by discussion within the communities themselves. Some, however, have been so severe and divisive that the community has been shattered, marriages broken, and individuals badly scarred. People involved have been forced to ask themselves whether the cause was simple human weakness, inadequate organization and knowledge, or a fundamental ethical blindspot within Zen itself.

Some of the sharpest problems recently faced by individuals and groups in the West have therefore clustered around the difficulty of understanding and dealing with authority in traditional Zen practice. Especially vexing is the question of a Zen teacher's authority over his or her disciples when the exercise of that authority seems to come into conflict with accepted patterns of everyday morality or common sense.

Zen stresses that enlightenment is the recognition of one's own inherent Buddha-nature, that there is nothing one needs to acquire from the outside. At the same time most seekers have found in practice that this realization does not come easily. They have looked for authentic guides, those who have themselves experienced enlightenment (*kenshō*) and can recognize it in others, perhaps even strike the spark that will allow the aspirant to achieve it himself. Zen teachers have little to impart or teach in any formal sense; they can only help individuals to experience buddhahood for themselves.

It was in this quest for true guides and authentic "mind-to-mind transmission" that hundreds of medieval Japanese monks went to China, wandered from master to master, and spent many years training in Chinese monasteries. It was in this search that countless Asian monks have wandered in their own countries like "clouds and water" from Zen hall to Zen hall. And it is in this same search that Western students of Zen continue to look for authentic teachers in the West and in Asia. Such a teacher can help deepen the experience drawn from *zazen* meditation, can assess whether *kōan* are truly mastered, and can distinguish self-deception from valid insight.

The importance of trust between master and disciple in Zen training is well expressed by Morinaga Roshi in the first chapter of this volume. Teacher and student are both involved in a deadly earnest struggle to recognize the Buddha-nature of oneself and all beings. This struggle is not undertaken lightly by those who choose to practice Zen, and it cannot be assumed lightly by those who are in the position of guiding others. It calls for absolute honesty and integrity on both sides. It demands faith on the part of the seeker, compassion and severity on the part of the teacher. One graphic illustration of the master-disciple relationship is the famous painting of the Chinese monk Hui-k'o offering his severed arm as a gesture of his determination to study under the Indian master Bodhidharma.

At the core of Zen training is the conviction that the realization of Buddha-nature cannot be achieved by rational understanding or conventional study, even study of the sutras. Over the centuries Chinese and Japanese Zen masters developed a variety of techniques to frustrate conceptualization and to deepen intuitive insight. These have included koans, shouts, blows, goads to spontaneous or nonrational behavior, and occasionally actions that seem to cut across common sense or morality. Recognizing the difficulty of conveying reality in words, Zen teachers have made use of such actions, as well as signs, metaphors, and paradoxes, to convey Zen experience as directly as possible. Zen masters may intentionally foster a Great Doubt in their students. They can be deceptive in order to point to deeper understanding.

Any means may seem justified in the effort to rouse their students to enlightenment. Zen practice therefore demands trust on the part of the student that such means only seem irrational due to the limitations of dualistic thinking, and that they are an expedient step on the way to self-realization. That is, the student must believe that the master's words or actions, however bizarre they may appear at times, are true in a deeper, yet-to-be-understood meaning.

For instance, in Zen we find admonitions to "die" or "kill": "If you meet the Buddha, kill the Buddha; if you meet the patriarchs, kill the patriarchs," or "if you meet your parents, kill your parents." Sometimes students may feel they are being asked, in the name of Zen, to "kill" things or relationships they value. Although they realize that these expressions are not intended to be taken literally, they are left with the problem of responding to them. How far is a person to go against conventional values in the pursuit of Zen? Where does one draw the line when a teacher gives instructions that are open to ambiguity? Instructions of this kind seem to take Zen outside the realm of conventional morality and common sense behavior. Trusting is not easy in these circumstances. It involves holding on to one's conviction that the guide is indeed a person of deep spiritual insight, that he would not make an unethical demand, and that his only concern is a compassionate desire to help the seeker come to awakening.

Though trust is an essential basis for the master-student relationship and for the deepening of practice, it does not have to be a blind trust involving the suspension or inversion of common sense and moral standards. There is a fine line between the kind of well-placed trust that leads to stronger practice and a misplaced trust that brings only pain. Occasionally one hears of Western students of Zen who have been hurt or frustrated by arbitrary, irrational, or immoral demands from their Zen teachers. In some cases the student may simply have failed to grasp a valid truth that was couched in indirect or ambivalent terms. In other cases, however, it is hard to avoid the conclusion that the teacher was behaving irresponsibly and confusing his own desires with his student's welfare and training in Zen. If it turns out that a person of supposed spiritual insight is all too human, or if a student comes to feel that a Zen master lacks the expected depth of insight, disillusion sets in. When the disillusion is directed only at that teacher, the student can seek another guide or another group. Sometimes, however, the disillusion is directed against Zen itself.

Because of the intensity of the master-student relationship in Zen and the authority invested in the master during training, there is always the possibility of an inadequate teacher knowingly or unwittingly abusing that authority. A teacher may undermine the student with such implied notions as: "Surely somebody who has attained enlightenment can't be suggesting something wrong or immoral," or "Since Zen does not proceed by rational methods, any behavior is licensed." The more dynamic the teacher, the stronger his or her influence on the student is likely to be. If this influence is exercised in the encouragement of true Zen insight then the effects may be splendid. If, however, such influence is warped or self-interested then it can only cause suffering for individuals and communities.

Part of the problem here is that individuals and groups, even normally skeptical people, sometimes invest Zen teachers with an almost divine aura. They assume that anyone in the role of Zen master must be a person of deep spiritual insight and compassion and that such a person can do or say no wrong. Such misconceptions have been rejected in these pages by Roshi Kapleau and others. Aspiring trainees would be wiser to maintain some of their natural skepticism. The relative newness of Zen in the West inevitably means that some people are placed in positions of spiritual leadership before they are ready. There are fully qualified teachers who have spent many years in intensive meditation, worked through hundreds of koans, and attained deep insight before assuming the heavy responsibility of guiding others. Such a person has also developed his sense of compassion through Zen training, and he has the psychological maturity to deal with the kinds of personal problems that students encounter.

There are those who have attained enlightenment and continue to deepen it as they teach—through zazen, reflection on koans, and practice in daily life. There are teachers who have achieved some degree of insight, yet have gone no further and let it rust. And there are a few who have had relatively shallow experience in meditation or koan study when they are placed in a position of authority.

A healthy skepticism need not be corrosive of essential trust and wholehearted practice. Students will not feel a need to question credentials if they are deepening their insight under severe and compassionate guidance. However, if they feel strain, or become troubled by the relationship, or repeatedly find themselves in situations of moral or psychological ambiguity with their teacher, they should simply exercise their normal critical faculties. After practicing wholeheartedly and giving a teacher the benefit of the doubt, a student may reach a point where it would be wise to seek another guide or another group. In any case, the teacher need not be confused with the teaching. The fact that a teacher turns out to have deep flaws, or that the chemistry of the relationship between student and teacher has not worked well, need not vitiate the promise of Zen training or preclude the possibility of training under another guide.

On the teacher's side should surely be two basic questions: Is disinterested guidance being offered? Is severity tempered with compassion? The master's role can only be to help students attain their own enlightenment, to point to the footsteps of the ox. It is then for the student to follow the footsteps, locate the ox, and master it. Zen stresses self-inquiry, independence of spirit, and the universality of buddhahood. A Zen teacher who, instead of liberating students, makes them dependent upon him has surely failed both his students and Zen.

Part of the difficulty in determining what is essential to the master's role and to Zen practice results from the inescapable fact that Zen is detached from a Buddhist context in the West. When Zen was carried to Japan from China in the twelfth century, as Professor Yampolsky's essay documents, it encountered an environment in which monks and lay practitioners had been exposed to Buddhism for centuries. They were familiar with Buddhist teaching and ethics, Buddhist philosophical speculation, Buddhist views of life and death, Buddhist monasticism and training methods. Although Zen mounted a challenge to the older schools of Buddhism and at times seemed iconoclastic, it was part of the whole Buddhist corpus in Japan, as it had been in China. Society and individuals had the requisite knowledge to place Zen in a broader religious context, notice what was novel about it, and see where it meshed with fundamental Buddhist teachings. They had standards by which to judge the behavior of monks and nuns, clarify the distinction between monastic and lay life, and evaluate the relationship between teachers and disciples. The existence of this larger context provided a subtle social control against individual or institutional excesses.

In the West, because there is no well-defined Sangha (religious community) or Buddhist context for the practice of Zen, there has been little lateral contact between the various groups. A Sangha embracing an institutional network of Zen communities, perhaps helping to integrate these groups with other Buddhist transmissions in the West, has still to develop. While things are going well this lack of communication is not felt to be a disadvantage. However, when a group experiences difficulties (as most groups will at one time or another) the absence of others' support and example is a drawback. Some of the Zen centers that have felt the sharpest internal difficulties have been those that are most isolated. While teachers and groups naturally want to maintain the distinctiveness of their lineage, protect the autonomy of their practice, and avoid organizational excess, they could all benefit from greater lateral communication and mutual support. Waywardness of the kind that has been evident recently can be quietly checked before it becomes chronic.

Ambiguity about the nature of the teacher's authority in Zen training has also been exaggerated by a confused use of titles and terms in Western Zen communities. Two particularly troublesome terms have been *rōshi* and *inka*. Roshi (literally, "elder teacher") does not have a precise single usage—the meaning varies between different branches of Zen in Japan, as Professor Foulk indicates herein. Sometimes it is a general term of respect for monks, especially older or senior monks; sometimes it is applied more narrowly to monks or laypeople with the insight to train others in Zen. In Japanese Rinzai Zen today the term is generally restricted to experienced masters of exceptional spiritual attainment who are designated to give *sanzen* (private instruction) to monks training in a formal monastic setting. There are few such roshis. Most have had at least thirty or forty years of Zen experience, and they are recognized by their teachers and peers as deeply enlightened. Zen in the West will come of age when it steadily produces such guides—whatever they are called—and can rely on them to train others.

There has sometimes been a tendency in the West to attribute the title of roshi, or some equivalent, to all Zen teachers or leaders of communities. Such titles have a talismanic ring to them, and people often assume that they apply in their most spiritual sense. But they do not confer wisdom or spiritual insight. Members of centers here can avoid investing their guides with undeserved, and usually unwanted, auras of sanctity if they will only look squarely at the depth of the person's insight, the effectiveness of his guidance, and his behavior within the community.

Inka refers to *inka shōmei*, the certification of an enlightenment experience and a recognition of the transmission of the Dharma from a teacher to a student. Like the term roshi, the usage of inka varies from one Zen lineage to another. Traditionally it is given by a master to a disciple who has completed his Zen training and is qualified to guide others. In East Asia this mind-to-mind transmission was marked symbolically by the handing down of such items as a robe, a bowl, a portrait of the master, or a written document. Zen masters have often chosen their own means of indicating the transmission of the Dharma to a disciple. In one sense, the inka system is no more than an institutional device for clarifying lines of succession. In a deeper

sense, it is a tangible confirmation that a spiritual transmission has been validated. While there may have been abuses at times, inka certificates are given grudgingly. On occasion a master may acknowledge somebody's enlightenment verbally so that no certificate passes.

In the West there are very few teachers who have actual inka certificates. There are a number, however, who have practiced Zen for many years, attained spiritual insight, and have been encouraged by their teachers to spread the Dharma and help others in Zen practice. Thus there may be qualified teachers without formal inka (and there may be inka-holders who are less capable as teachers). The future of Zen in the West will necessarily rest on the acquisition and extension of full and authentic Zen transmission. In the long run there must be true "roshis" and true bearers of "inka," whether they have titles, certificates, or not.

Following the enthusiasms of the 1960s, when Zen became something of a popular cult and universal catchword, it is now less in the public eye. Those who were merely toying with it dropped away, and more serious practitioners remain. The changing political and social winds of the 1970s and 1980s have been much less favorable than the liberal sixties to spiritual practices like Zen. Though centers continue and new groups are formed, the mood at the moment in American Zen circles is one of consolidation and the search for bearings. It is not surprising that problems of authority, group organization, and adaptation to a new culture have become more urgent. Though occasionally very painful, these problems need not be destructive to communities or individuals if they are handled sensitively and sincerely. Sometimes answers will be found in closer adherence to the traditional ideals of Chinese, Japanese, or Korean Zen practice. Sometimes new answers, more appropriate to the conditions facing Zen in Western society, will have to be sought. Out of this process, which is already under way, will come a stronger, surer Zen practice. It will be a genuine synthesis, drawing on Asian roots but realizing a universality that transcends both East and West.

Contributors

Martin Collcutt, Professor in the Department of East Asian Studies at Princeton University, is the author of *Five Mountains: The Rinzai Zen Monastic Institution in Medieval Japan* (1981).

T. Griffith Foulk, Assistant Professor in the Department of Asian Languages and Cultures at the University of Michigan, is currently working on a history of Zen monastic codes.

Philip Kapleau is Roshi of the Zen Center of Rochester, New York. He has written *The Three Pillars of Zen* (1965), *The Wheel of Death* (1971), *Zen: Dawn in the West* (1979), *To Cherish All Life* (1981), and a forthcoming work on death, dying, and rebirth.

Kenneth Kraft, Assistant Professor in the Department of Oriental Studies at the University of Pennsylvania, is completing a book on Daitō, a Zen master of medieval Japan.

Albert Low, Director and Teacher of the Zen Centre of Montreal, Canada, has published *Zen and Creative Management* (1976) and *The Iron Cow of Zen* (1985). His *Invitation to the Practice of Zen* is in progress.

John R. McRae, Postdoctoral Fellow at the John King Fairbank Center for East Asian Research, Harvard University, is the author of *The Northern School and the Formation of Early Ch'an Buddhism* (1986).

Contributors

Morinaga Sōkō is Roshi of Daishuin temple in Kyoto, Japan, and President of Hanazono University, also in Kyoto. His works include *Zenkai ichiran* [*One Wave on the Ocean of Zen*] (1987).

Sheng-Yen is Master of the Ch'an Meditation Center, Elmhurst, New York, and Director of the Chung-Hwa Institute of Buddhist Studies, Taiwan. He has written *Getting the Buddha Mind* (1982) and *The Poetry of Enlightenment* (1987).

Eido T. Shimano is Abbot of the Zen Studies Society in New York City. He is the author of *Golden Wind* (1979), co-author of *Namu Dai Bosa* (1976), and editor of *Like a Dream, Like a Fantasy* (1978).

Burton Watson is Adjunct Professor in the Department of East Asian Languages and Cultures at Columbia University. He has published more than twenty works, including *Early Chinese Literature* (1962), *The Complete Works of Chuang Tzu* (1968), and *Chinese Lyricism* (1971).

Philip Yampolsky, Professor in the Department of East Asian Languages and Cultures at Columbia University, is the author of *The Platform Sutra of The Sixth Patriarch* (1967) and *The Zen Master Hakuin* (1971).

Notes

Introduction

1. Hakuin Ekaku (1686–1769) in Philip B. Yampolsky, *The Zen Master Hakuin: Selected Writings* (New York: Columbia University Press, 1971), pp. 121–122.
2. Bernard Tetsugen Glassman Sensei, in Peter Matthiessen, *Nine-Headed Dragon River* (Boston: Shambhala, 1986), pp. 125–126.
3. Zenkei Shibayama, *Zen Comments on the Mumonkan* (New York: The New American Library, 1974), p. 207 (with minor changes).
4. Daisetz T. Suzuki, *Essentials of Zen Buddhism* (London: Rider & Co., 1963), p. 242.
5. Luis O. Gómez, "Expectations and Assertions: Perspectives for Growth and Adaptation in Buddhism," *Zen Buddhism Today: Annual Report of the Kyoto Zen Symposium I* (Kyoto: Kyoto Seminar for Religious Philosophy, 1983), p. 33.
6. Ōkubo Dōshū, ed. *Dōgen Zenji zenshū* (Tokyo: Chikuma Shobō, 1969–70), vol. 1, p. 405.
7. G. B. Sansom, *Japan: A Short Cultural History* (Tokyo: Charles E. Tuttle, rev. ed., 1974), p. 340.
8. John C. Maraldo, "What Do We Study When We Study Zen?" *Zen Buddhism Today*, p. 71.
9. Takakusu Junjirō et al., *Taishō shinshū daizōkyō* (Tokyo: Daizō Shuppan, 1924–32), vol. 80, p. 332c.

10. Kenneth L. Kraft, trans. "Musō Kokushi's *Dialogues in a Dream:* Selections," *The Eastern Buddhist* 14:1 (Spring 1981), p. 92.
11. Maraldo, "What Do We Study When We Study Zen?" p. 82.
12. The first chapter originally appeared in Japanese in 1982 (see Chapter 1, note 2).

My Struggle to Become a Zen Monk

1. *Passages Deploring Deviations of Faith* (*Tannishō*) is a summary of the teachings of Shinran (1173–1262), founder of the True Pure Land sect of Japanese Buddhism.
2. The full text of this essay was originally published in volume form as *Zenji no seikatsu* (Toyama: Toyama-ken Kyōikuiinkai, 1982) and in English as *Pointers to Insight: The Life of a Zen Monk* (London: Zen Centre, 1985), translated by James Stokes. The present abridged version has been adapted with the author's and the Zen Centre's permission.

The Private Encounter with the Master

1. Philip Kapleau, *The Three Pillars of Zen* (Garden City: Anchor Press/Doubleday, rev. ed., 1980), p. 214.
2. Philip Kapleau, *Zen: Dawn in the West* (Garden City: Anchor Press/Doubleday, 1979), pp. 34–35.
3. Heinrich Zimmer, *Philosophies of India* (Princeton: Princeton University Press, 1969), p. 544.
4. Ken Wilber, *Eye to Eye: The Quest for the New Paradigm* (Garden City: Anchor Press/Doubleday, 1983), p. 265.
5. Philip B. Yampolsky, *The Zen Master Hakuin: Selected Writings* (New York: Columbia University Press, 1971), p. 137.
6. Ibid., p. 137.

Zen Koans

1. Many of the koans and Western passages quoted in this chapter are drawn from memory, and I have not attempted to provide full bibliographic citations for them. I have also taken the liberty of

using the Japanese pronunciation of the names of Chinese Zen masters, because those are the names most familiar to me from my own training.

2. Zenkei Shibayama, *Zen Comments on the Mumonkan* (New York: Harper & Row, 1974), p. 125.
3. Thomas & J. C. Cleary, *The Blue Cliff Record* (Boulder: Prajñā, 1977), p. 531.
4. Katsuki Sekida, *Two Zen Classics: Mumonkan & Hekiganroku* (New York and Tokyo: John Weatherhill, 1977), p. 131.
5. Ruth F. Sasaki, *The Record of Lin-chi* (Kyoto: Institute for Zen Studies, 1975), p. 57 (slightly modified).
6. Shibayama, *Zen Comments on the Mumonkan*, p. 272.
7. Sekida, *Two Zen Classics*, p. 55 (slightly modified).
8. Sasaki, *The Record of Lin-chi*, pp. 11–12.
9. Sekida, *Two Zen Classics*, p. 287.
10. Shibayama, *Zen Comments on the Mumonkan*, p. 181 (slightly modified).
11. Sekida, *Two Zen Classics*, p. 49 (slightly modified).
12. Shibayama, *Zen Comments on the Mumonkan*, p. 54.
13. Sekida, *Two Zen Classics*, p. 47.

Master Hakuin's Gateway to Freedom

1. Philip Kapleau, *Zen: Dawn in the West* (Garden City: Anchor Press/Doubleday, 1979), pp. 182–183 (slightly modified).
2. Reiho Masunaga, *The Sōtō Approach to Zen* (Tokyo: Layman's Buddhist Society, 1958), p. 81.
3. Shunryu Suzuki, *Zen Mind, Beginner's Mind* (Tokyo: John Weatherhill, 1970), p. 26.
4. H. Wildon-Carr, *Henri Bergson—The Philosophy of Change* (London: T. C. & E. C. Jack, 1911), pp. 28–29.
5. Swami Prabhavananda and Christopher Isherwood, *The Song of God* (London: Phoenix House, 1947), p. 116.

6. James Robinson, ed. *The Nag Hammadi Library* (San Francisco: Harper & Row, 1977), p. 126.
7. *Revised Standard Version Bible* (Grand Rapids: Zondervan Bible Publishers, 1971), p. 517.
8. Iwamoto Yasunami, "The Salvation of the Unsaveable," *The Eastern Buddhist* 10:1 (May 1977), p. 28.

Zen Poetry

1. See Philip Yampolsky, *The Platform Sutra of the Sixth Patriarch* (New York: Columbia University Press, 1967), pp. 128–33. For the third line of Hui-neng's verse I have followed the reading that appears in Sung and post-Sung versions of the text. The earliest text, that found at Tun-huang and dating from the T'ang, reads: "Buddha-nature is always clean and pure."
2. Terada Tōru, *Gidō Shūshin, Zekkai Chūshin; Nihon shijinsen*, vol. 24 (Tokyo: Chikuma Shobō, 1977), p. 65.
3. Katō Shūichi and Yanagida Seizan, *Ikkyū; Nihon no Zengoroku*, vol. 12 (Tokyo: Kōdansha, 1978), p. 188.
4. Harada Ryūmon, *Jakushitsu Genkō* (Tokyo: Shunshūsha, 1979), p. 218.
5. *Bukkyō bungakushū; Koten Nihon bungaku zenshū*, vol. 15 (Tokyo: Chikuma Shobō, 1961), p. 286.
6. Harada Ryūmon, *op. cit.*, p. 132.
7. Shibayama Zenkei, *Gōko fūgetsushū* (Osaka: Sōgensha, 1969), p. 112.
8. Ibid., p. 46.
9. Harada Ryūmon, *op.cit.*, p. 82.
10. Daisetz Teitaro Suzuki, trans. *The Lankāvatāra Sutra* (London: Routledge & Kegan Paul, 1932), pp. 91, 44.
11. Ogawa Tamaki, ed. *Tōdai no shijin: sono denki* (Tokyo: Daishūkan Shoten, 1975), pp. 625–35.
12. *Po Hsiang-shan shih Ch'ang-ch'ing chi* 16.
13. *Po Hsiang-shan shih hou-chi* 16.
14. *Po-shih Ch'ang-ch'ing chi* 70.

15. Kitamura Sawakichi, *Gozan bungaku shikō* (Tokyo: Tōyamabō, 1941), p. 695.
16. Kageki Hideo, *Gozan shishi no kenkyū* (Tokyo: Kasama Shoin, 1977), p. 356.
17. Kitamura Sawakichi, *op. cit.*, p. 258.
18. John Stevens, *Mountain Tasting: Zen Haiku by Santōka Taneda* (Tokyo: John Weatherhill, 1980), p. 24.

The Story of Early Ch'an

1. Philip B. Yampolsky, *The Platform Sutra of the Sixth Patriarch* (New York: Columbia University Press, 1967), p. 129 (slightly modified).
2. For consistency, I have used Professor Watson's translations of the two "mind verses." The one slight variation (third line of second verse) figures later in this essay.
3. D. T. Suzuki, *The Zen Doctrine of No-mind* (London: Rider & Co., 1949), p. 22.

The Development of Japanese Zen

1. The important figures of Japanese Zen usually have two monastic names and one or more honorary titles. By custom, some are better known by their first monastic name (*Dōgen* Kigen), some by their second name (Dainichi *Nōnin*), and some by their title (*Daitō* Kokushi). In this essay a person's most familiar name will be given preference.
2. Nishi Giyū and Fujimoto Chitō, trans. *Honchō kōsō den; Kokuyaku issaikyō*, vol. 89 (Tokyo: Daitō Shuppan, 1961), p. 272–73.
3. Yanagida Seizan, *Chūsei Zenke no shisō; Nihon shisō taikei*, vol. 16 (Tokyo: Iwanami Shoten, 1972), p. 41.
4. Norman Waddell and Masao Abe, trans. "Dōgen's *Bendōwa,*" *The Eastern Buddhist* 4:1 (May 1971), pp. 144–145.
5. Martin Collcutt, *Five Mountains: The Rinzai Zen Monastic Institution in Medieval Japan* (Cambridge: Harvard University Press, 1981), p. 67.

6. Kenneth L. Kraft, trans. "Musō Kokushi's *Dialogues in a Dream*: Selections," *The Eastern Buddhist* 14:1 (Spring 1981), p. 92.
7. James H. Sanford, *Zen-man Ikkyū* (Chico, CA: Scholars Press, 1981), p. 166.
8. Philip B. Yampolsky, *The Zen Master Hakuin: Selected Writings* (New York: Columbia University Press, 1971), p. 49 (slightly modified).

The Zen Institution in Modern Japan

1. Based on Bunkachō, ed. *Shūkyō nenkan* (Tokyo: Gyōsei, 1985), pp. 160–162.

Recent Developments in North American Zen

1. Katy Butler, "Events are the Teacher," *The Coevolution Quarterly*, Winter 1983, p. 115.
2. Peter Matthiessen, *Nine-headed Dragon River* (Boston: Shambhala, 1986), p. 228.
3. Wendy Egyoku Nakao, "Dharma Dialogue: Taking Care of Zen Practice," *The Ten Directions* (Los Angeles: Zen Center of Los Angeles), 6:1, Spring 1985, p. 15.
4. Butler, "Events are the Teacher," p. 121.
5. Robert Aitken et al., "Social Action Beyond Hope and Fear," *The Vajradhatu Sun* (Boulder: Vajradhatu), 8:6, Aug.–Sept. 1986, p. 11.
6. "Who Is It Who Wants To Be Ordained?," *Zen Bow* (Rochester: The Zen Center), 11:1, Aug. 1978, p. 9 (speaker not identified).
7. Jan Chozen Soule, "Taking Realization Into Everyday Life," *Primary Point* (Cumberland, RI: Kwan Um Zen School), 2:1, Feb. 1985, p. 6.
8. Albert Low, "Issues and Problems: Reflections on Questions Raised at the Conference on Zen in North America" (unpublished manuscript, 1986), p. 19.

9. Martin Collcutt, *Five Mountains: The Rinzai Zen Monastic Institution in Medieval Japan* (Cambridge: Harvard University Press, 1981), pp. 188–189.
10. "The Balancing of American Buddhism," *Primary Point*, 3:1, Feb. 1986, p. 6 (transcription slightly modified).
11. Ralph Harper Silver, producer, "Sunseed" (New Age Productions, 1973); passage paraphrased slightly.
12. "Interview with Sensei Bodhin," *Zen Bow*, 8:2, Autumn 1986, p. 5.
13. Lincoln Rhodes, "Integrity and Family Life," *Primary Point*, 2:2, May 1985, p. 3.
14. Thomas Merton, *Zen and the Birds of Appetite* (New York: New Directions, 1968), pp. 33, 47.
15. Samu Sunim, "A Brief History of Zen Buddhism in North America," *Spring Wind* (Toronto: The Zen Lotus Society), March 1986, p. 34. The historian Arnold Toynbee has made a similar assertion.
16. Philip Kapleau, *Zen: Dawn in the West* (Garden City: Anchor Press/Doubleday, 1979), p. 269.
17. Seung Sahn, "A Time of Complete Transformation," *Primary Point*, 3:2, June 1986, p. 2.
18. Matthiessen, *Nine-headed Dragon River*, p. 126.
19. *Newsletter* (Springwater, NY: Springwater Center), Oct. 1986, p. 14.
20. "OL' MAN RIVER" written by Jerome Kern and Oscar Hammerstein II. Copyright © 1927 T. B. Harms Company. Copyright Renewed. (c/o The Welk Music Group, Santa Monica, California, 90401). International Copyright Secured. All Rights Reserved. Used by Permission.
21. Samu Sunim, "A Brief History of Zen Buddhism in North America," p. 20.
22. Shigetsu Sasaki, "Excerpts from *Our Lineage,*" *Wind Bell* (San Francisco: Zen Center), 8:1–2, Fall 1969, p. 6 (translation slightly modified).

Index

Index